Burnt Offerings

Burnt Offerings

The Art of Politics and the Consequences of Freedom

Guy ———— Finally finished it.
Hope you enjoy it. Now I have to
find a way to get others interested
Floyd

BOOK 1

Floyd Sours

Copyright © 2010 by Floyd Sours.

Library of Congress Control Number:		2010906656
ISBN:	Hardcover	978-1-4500-9985-1
	Softcover	978-1-4500-9929-5
	Ebook	978-1-4500-9986-8

All rights reserved. No part of this book may be reproduced or transmitted in any form or by any means, electronic or mechanical, including photocopying, recording, or by any information storage and retrieval system, without permission in writing from the copyright owner.

This book was printed in the United States of America.

To order additional copies of this book, contact:
Xlibris Corporation
1-888-795-4274
www.Xlibris.com
Orders@Xlibris.com
79311

Six Blind Men and an Elephant

It was six men of Indostan to learning much inclined, who went to see the elephant though all of them were blind, that each of them by observation might satisfy his mind.

The first approached the elephant and happening to fall against his broad and sturdy side, at once began to bawl: "God bless me!" but the elephant is very like a wall.

The second, feeling of the tusk, cried, "Ho! What have we here, so very round and smooth and sharp? To me 'tis mighty clear, this wonder of an elephant is very like a spear!"

"The third approached the animal, and happening to take the squirming trunk within his hands, thus boldly up and spake: I see," quoth he, "the elephant is very like a snake!"

The fourth reached out an eager hand, and felt about the knee. "What most this wondrous beast is like is mighty plain," quoth he; "'tis clear enough the elephant is very like a tree."

The fifth, who chanced to touch the ear, said: "E'en the blindest man can tell what this resembles most: deny the fact who can this marvel of an elephant is very like a fan!"

The sixth no sooner had begun about the beast to grope, than, seizing on the swinging tail that fell within his scope, "I see," quoth he, "the elephant is very like a rope!"

And so these men of Indostan disputed loud and long, each in his own opinion exceeding stiff and strong, though each was partly in the right, and all were in the wrong!

So oft in theologic wars, the disputants, I ween, rail on in utter ignorance of what each other mean, and prate about an elephant not one of them has seen!

—John Godfrey Saxe

Contents

Acknowledgments 9

Preface 11

1   Introduction 15

2   Freedom 18

3   Equality 26

4   Constraints 33

5   The Ides of March 42

6   Examples 47

7   Good and Evil 69

8   Bad Judgment 77

9   Losing the Magic 85

10 Synopsis 92

Bibliography 101

Appendix: Sources for Graphs 1, 2, & 3 105

INDEX 107

Acknowledgments

Although this book has been long in coming, it would not be available at all if a large number of people had not helped with their various talents. It began as a solitary project at the early age of eighteen when I headed off to college. No one else in my immediate family had gone to college, except my mother. She completed two years and then got married.

While I did not do so well at first, I did learn to value reading and thinking. Somewhere in my college career, I wrote out four goals that I wished to achieve. One of them was to write a book. This book is the fulfillment of that goal. I wish to thank my parents and my extended family for teaching me the value of overcoming adversity and persistence as I've led my life.

I also want to thank my wife, Carol, who diligently encouraged me to write, even when I was too busy with other things. She also read the manuscript through the years while constantly critiquing it when the ideas in it were too intellectual or just unclear. The rest of my current family consists of our children, who all grew up and started families of their own. They too endeavored to help in whatever way that they could. I certainly want to thank David and Lynn Sours, Frank and Amy Dosch, and Jerry and Lisa Feldman for all the encouragement.

There were others, who also were family, that helped as well. Kasey Feldman, our granddaughter and graduate student, helped me acquire data for the manuscript. Of course, there is a very special thanks to our other granddaughter, Lacey Dotson, for using us as babysitters for her daughter, Lexus. Our great-granddaughter, at the age of two and three, was a delightful break from the drudgery of writing. Carol, Lexus, and I spent hours being spontaneous, as we danced and sang together. Without the presence of her natural inquisitiveness, unspoiled behavior and pure innocence, I don't believe this book could have been written.

Of course, there were other friends, mostly professionals, who helped in more direct ways. The earliest 500-page draft of the manuscript was read in part by Keli Yee, PsyD, who asked if I really believed what I have written while offering critique in grammar. Later, other professionals lent their talent to critiquing a shortened version. They are listed as follows: Lee Roach, PhD, Don McIntire, PhD, Robert Lowder, PhD, Guy Melvin, PhD, and John Bohley, LISW, DPA. I would be remiss if I did not mention my brother-in-law and computer guru, Terry Rogers, MBA who spent much time explaining Windows office word and critiquing text. His contribution was perhaps the most important one for the finished product.

There are others, such as Dr. Francis Fukuyama at Johns Hopkins University, who allowed me access to his graphs and its data from the book *The Great Disruption*. I would also like to thank John Webster, a morning show staple of Cleveland radio for years and the past co-owner of a business called The Reel Thing. John is my cousin and good friend, who is now retired. He read parts of the manuscript stating very positive things about it. He really kept my spirits up when I needed reinforcements. There is also Katie Crabtree Thomas of the Ohio Psychological Association who was kind enough to help enlist several psychologists to critique the manuscript. To Katie and the others who provided critique, thank you very much.

I would be remiss if I didn't comment on the lack of big organized university and corporate support. I could not help notice that almost all of the successful books that I have read involve support by large organizations that network with authors that have name recognition. Alas, this book came about largely as a solitary project over many years. This author has had little of that kind of support largely because this was an individual project. It is my hope that, with the publishing of this book, larger organizations and name recognition will follow.

Preface

About six years ago, I began to have time on my hands because my small business had become successful. More than that, my wife was the office manager, and my staff was serene and working hard. I knew, throughout my life, that I wanted to write an original, true nonfiction book about America. However, work was always interfering.

At other times, my mind was too cluttered with other more immediate thoughts. Still, I constantly read rather scholarly works, and I kept a running diary that I called "Random Thoughts." There certainly were times when I felt a certain uneasiness as the ideas presented in other people's books did not quite explain what I was seeing in the real world around me.

When success lifted the stresses of the workplace from me, I immediately began to read. I read rather scholarly works by Dr. Eric Fromm, Dr. David Reisman, Dr. Orlando Patterson, Dr. Theodore Lowi, and Dr. Francis Fukuyama to name a few. I took new notes from some of these books while others were reread several times. The point is that a great deal of new information erupted into my consciousness as I began to write. In fact, I could not stop writing. For all practical purposes, I was obsessed but satisfied that I was doing something that I had wanted to do all my life.

As page after page unfolded, my mind buzzed with intrusive thoughts that helped organize the written material. It was as if an invisible stranger was guiding my hand. I wrote hour after hour, day after day, and month after month until four years had passed. Work and family became secondary as I continued to be preoccupied with the manuscript most of the time. At last, the entire manuscript of about 500 pages was finished, but, alas, that was only the beginning.

It was clear to me that there were several very important ideas present in that first rough draft. Indeed, it seemed to have a certain amount of predictive ability when it came to American politics. However, it was also clear that it was too complicated, too long, and involved many grammatical mistakes.

It was quite necessary to use Occam's razor and the law of parsimony to simplify and clarify this monotonous tome.

One or two years later, after many revisions, it was complete. The book now began with a dialogue about the kinds of freedom and their history. The point was made that in America, today, we are motivated by the belief in one kind of freedom. Because democratic people only know one kind of freedom, they look at things in a particular way. By knowing and believing in three kinds of freedom, people are forced to look at things in a quite different way. That is particularly true of politics and government.

Looking at American politics through the prism of different kinds of freedom gives the reader an entirely new view regarding many political and social problems. For instance, the conventional modern view of equal freedom for illegal immigrants, criminals, and responsible citizens is based on the idea of personal freedom. It presumes that each of them should always be treated equally. On the other hand, another kind of older freedom gives preference to responsible citizens who abide by the law but punishes criminals and illegal immigrants for breaking the law.

This different view presumes inequality between responsible citizens on the one hand and lawbreakers on the other. The two views are quite different from one another. Politicians in modern America seem unable to grasp the idea that governments have traditionally awarded freedom to those good citizens who are law abiding. Conversely, criminals and illegal immigrants were punished for breaking the law.

There is also a myriad of dialogue that proposes that politicians and our government are now out of control, corrupt, and unable to use good judgment. It is proposed that national and international responsibilities, expanding technological know-how, and polarized political ideologies have left politics and government far behind. The result is a bunch of rigid, carping politicians who often make bad decisions. Yet those same politicians are grandiose and sure that they know something the rest of us do not know. Since our politicians cannot experience the satisfaction of good decisions and responsible action, they regress into corruption and coercion.

The benefit of theorizing on political behavior using a standard outside of the political arena provides the possibility of an unbiased objective view of politics and government. Hence, politics tends to produce an unsettling feeling in the general population because it seems that there are no answers to political and social problems. Only confusion, corruption, and coercion are visible, as our politicians manipulate and deceive us. The insertion of an independent means to analyze political behavior can remove age-old bias and produce possible real solutions to problems.

In this book, several seemingly impossible current political conflicts are presented in a new way. Further, the inclusion of the three types of freedom makes problem solving on many other issues potentially solvable as well. The use of a new standard for viewing our culture and politics simply defines three kinds of freedom where Americans currently believe in but one kind.

Freedom has been such a basic construct in our country that its effect on the way people and politicians think has not even been examined. When it is discovered and believed, the way we think about our culture is altered. In this book, there is also speculation about where we might be headed in the future politically.

I should also mention that the name "Burnt Offerings" for this book was meant to be a kind of dark but selfless narrative that could return to the reader a much better understanding of our culture. In the writing of this diatribe initially, the sole purpose was to be objective and to learn from the experience. However, as time passed and the ideas conflicted and morphed into new levels of awareness, the end results amazed even me. This book really took on a life of its own, leaving this author to wonder how a work like this could be produced that did not necessarily reflect his own beliefs.

April 13, 2010
Floyd Sours

1

Introduction

In the valley of the blind, the sighted are cripples.

—Anonymous

Beware! This is a book for individual thinkers and doers who are striving to better understand the culture in which they live. A clear statement is presented that makes those seeking freedom and equality for all, the unintended creators of harm in a world that is out of control. This is not a book for ideologues, but individual independent thinkers and doers may get an unintended rush from its content. Regardless of what you think you believe the recipes put forth in this book produce a highly toxic stew that eventually ends up analyzing American politics. So open your mind to a different way of thinking that will allow you to visualize our world in a new and better way.

What follows is a compendium of analyses of mostly famous scholarly authors. For the past half a century, America has experienced unprecedented prosperity that is attributed to unparalleled technological innovation fueled by the spirit of freedom. While we bask in the knowledge of prosperity and freedom, many of the authors I have read have identified cultural problems in America.

Those problems are backed up with examples, reasonable arguments, and statistical data. This cauldron of problems and conflicting ideas is morphed into practical solutions by combining similar themes. The end result is a clear argument that our pursuit of freedom and equality is too simple and has many flaws. The truth is much of our modern world has developed from old traditional inequalities.

These inequalities are so basic that we do not identify them as separate and different. Still, they are a necessary part of the way we think and interact with one another. It is quite necessary for inequalities to exist for doctor–patient, teacher–student, policeman–criminal, parent–child, politician–voter, and employer–employee relationships. In trying to equalize those relationships, we diminish the effectiveness of our schools, courts, medical treatment, government agencies, workplaces, and families.

Through the years, I have read, saved my books, and written short vignettes and random thoughts to myself. All of these were kept in boxes and old suitcases. Wherever I went, my books and writings traipsed along. The books were usually popular, nonfictional, and intellectual, although that was not always the case. Recently, with a successful private practice, I have found time to read, think, and surf the Internet.

I have found that much of my reading was filled with conflicting, detailed ideas that lacked any clear, overall answers to our current cultural problems. The Internet also provided highly detailed portrayals of cultural problems. Our experts, with the perspective of a jeweler, described the same problems time and again. To my way of thinking, no real global theories were offered. Some of my thoughts surprised even me . . . as I began to write. The result is this book, which concerns itself with modern America and its veiled cultural biases regarding equal freedom for all.

I personally believe our secular society no longer believes in good or bad; only equality. In our modern society, belief in good and bad means inequality: that good people are not equal to bad people. This idea of good and bad being unequal has been part of the motivating force for America since the beginning and has rightfully been referred to as part of the spirit of America; its *Zeitgeist*. More recently, equality in tandem with our concept of freedom has more or less replaced the older, more traditional ideas. This book contains numerous examples of inequalities that are under pressure to become equalities. Some of these inequalities are beneficial and some are harmful.

There are other revelations in this book that are worthy of mention, but the central theme lies in the relationship between inequality and equality. Aside from the obvious benefits of freedom and equality, the question of whether they are related to high crime rates, impoverished education, high rates of mental illness, and increasingly poor judgment in government is also discussed. In these discussions, hard statistical data is offered when available. In its absence, logical explanations are presented.

Much of this book is dedicated to the unspoken public proposition that too much of prosperity and a free ride can corrupt. The corruption we see everyday in the news seems to originate in every one of us as we feign goodness while imbibing in the pleasures of narcissism and harm. The premise is that our politicians are more corrupt and harmfully manipulative than the rest of us because they have fewer constraints placed upon them. They are free.

Another underlying concern, on which much of this book is based, is that people seek physical and mental pleasure and disclaim much of those things that are unpleasant. Cultural rewards give pleasure to individuals, but punishments are unpleasant. For people, activities that involve work or require discipline are often thought of as unpleasant. Many, without guidance, find thinking about the world around them unpleasant because the world seems chaotic and meaningless. The result is that they become anxious and feel lonelier.

Yet in order to become more mature and wise, one must somehow understand that chaos and give meaning to it. We need to overcome adversity by understanding. This book proposes that no civilization can show individuals the way through adversity, for it is an unpleasant experience that most people avoid. Those who become mature are rare. Only they are truly free: internally and externally. Society can only offer superficial rewards and punishment. No matter what occurs externally, your thoughts are free.

There are a lot of other themes and premises that are offered in this literary odyssey. If you would like to cohort with me in this adventure, read on!

2

Freedom

Freedom, although it has brought (modern man) independence
and rationality, has made him isolated and anxious.

—Eric Fromm

Many years ago, while I was reading books regularly and trying to write,
I found certain books really meaningful and exciting. The cultural problems
in those books appeared as common themes as I read those books again in
a modern context. For me today, these themes are the real problems in the
real world. These problems, to me, are the harmful consequences of equal
freedom for all in western civilization. Of course, there are many powerful
benefits to freedom, but that is not the theme of this book.

Although conflicts rage on in the popular media regarding whether
these harmful problems even exist, this book assumes they exist because
of the overwhelming evidence. What is new in this book is the introduction
of the idea that these problems are really created by our outdated, overly
simple ideas about freedom and equality. In this book, the emphasis is on
equality as a cultural problem that operates in tandem with loosened cultural
constraints. Both of these twin towers of conflict create much of our current
cultural problems.

This chapter will explore the different kinds of freedom and point out
that we really acknowledge only one kind of freedom today. The two kinds
of older freedom are sovereign and civic freedoms while personal freedom
is our modern choice. These two older kinds of freedom are associated with
inequality and are regarded with suspicion. On the other hand, our modern
personal freedom is related to equality.

In order to make some sense of the kinds of freedom, I have engaged in a quick discourse on all three kinds of freedom, which contain the two older kinds of freedom. First, it is clear that sovereign and civic freedoms have been mostly present in authoritarian governments where little or no equality existed. On the other hand, democracy is described as embodying personal freedom in tandem with equality.

By grouping these problems in this way, I have been able to make a pretty convincing case for personal freedom and infer equality as the source of considerable ongoing harm as well as benefits. Still, no American whom I know thinks there is any harm associated with our current freedom. Contrary to public opinion, this harm looks like a secret cultural bias of immense proportions.

Different Faces of Freedom

Freedom had likely developed from its opposite, slavery. Societies in antiquity used slave labor as an economic force to get things done. In the absence of modern science, technology, and work ethic, the brutal reality was that slaves were the engine that made things go. In order to fully understand how such a system could be embraced by so many people everywhere, one must understand that interpersonally few successful human relationships existed in antiquity. These failures in human relationships were documented in the multitude of Greek and Roman tragedies. The people held extreme intense opinions, poorly developed language skills, and disastrous public relations. It is all reflected in the literature and plays of the day.

Viewing slavery as a right without any thought of its harm is not unlike our current opinion of considering progress and freedom as entirely beneficial. Progress today is marketed as a way to solve human problems through technology. People who believe in progress as a solution sell it as a great benefit while dismissing any harm. These progressives have general recent history on their side, insisting that more economic prosperity is just around the corner. They see prosperity as a never-ending succession of benefits. Nowhere do they consider that human progress may be cyclical, with our current problem-solving ability peaking out. Likewise, there is no consideration of the harm done to our culture by the forces of progress.

Yet today there are generally more successful interpersonal relationships, individual opinions are less obstructive, and public opinion seems less radical when compared to antiquity. Of course, the exception to that statement is our current cultural crisis and great recession. Although we still have our interpersonal failures as reflected in our popular novels and stories of the day, life does not seem as tragic as it was in the past. Good endings in personal relationships appear to be more frequent. Perhaps then, western civilization has made some progress after all over the years.

Dr. Patterson, the author of the book *Freedom* (1991), examines in depth the relationship between the kinds of freedom and slavery. In fact, he makes an excellent argument for freedom developing from slavery. He also states, "freedom . . . was first socially constructed in ancient Athens." In his book, he describes the kinds of freedom as follows:

- Sovereign freedom . . . is simply the power (of a sovereign) to act as (he) pleases, regardless of the wishes of others.
- Personal freedom . . . is the capacity (for individuals) to do as one pleases, insofar as one can.
- Civic freedom . . . is the capacity of adult members of a community to participate in its life and governance.

He emphasized that these kinds of freedom can alternate together or independently, but if all three are present and are resonating together as "a harmonious whole," they represent what we perceive as ideal freedom.

It is clear that Dr. Patterson understood that there are different kinds of freedom. The first is sovereign freedom that consists of freeing one individual who has absolute authority to govern. That one free person as ruler is then expected to provide a more prosperous and satisfying life for those who are not free. The second type of freedom is called personal freedom. It is more of a modern phenomenon that theoretically involves equal freedom for all. The third kind of freedom is civic freedom. It means that all free citizens are given special privileges or partial freedom in so far as they obey the law. In the case of civic freedom, more people are able to be partially free compared to sovereign freedom.

The modern idea of personal freedom contains many different official definitions, with all involving the absence of oppressive constraint. There is another element that is sometimes included that stresses the ability of an individual to stand alone while exercising his own choices. The latter definition is not always included, leaving the definition often focusing solely on the lack of external constraint.

In modern America, there is a popular version of freedom that has distorted the original meaning of personal freedom. The popular, often unarticulated, vulgarized view means the ability of everyone to think, say, or do whatever and whenever one wants. It is a gross simplification of the official definition that I first heard as a psychologist in one of our prisons. In both definitions, the idea of loosening constraints is central.

There are many people today protesting causes, in the spirit of freedom, that try to justify blindly removing constraints on individuals and groups.

The idea of personal responsibility through choice is completely lost by many people. In order to better understand how we arrived at such an idea down through the ages, it is necessary to provide some background regarding freedom and how we lost our way.

Dr. Patterson observed that constraints are involved in sovereign and civic freedoms, while the absence of constraint is central to modern personal freedom as well as the overly simple popular view. Originally, in the case of freedom, Dr. Patterson argued that the concept of freedom developed with and from slavery. But both masters and slaves are opposites and the old ancient culture only perceived the differences between them. Today, we perceive masters and slaves together in a relationship of opposites. However, we now call them predators and victims.

A study of the relationship between these opposites, including some of their similarities, reveals a much clearer and changed view of freedom that focuses on the loosening of constraints. It is this emphasis on the removal of constraints that is often assumed in our present culture without much thought toward the consequences. This emphasis is closely associated with personal and popular freedoms.

In an earlier book titled *Slavery and Social Death* (1982), Dr. Patterson focused on slavery, what it is and was, as contrasted to freedom. For instance, he states "those who most denied freedom (masters), as well as those to whom it was most denied (slaves), were the very persons most alive to it (freedom)."

Both of these books provide a wonderful and imaginative read that may enlighten and teach any honest reader about the connections between freedom and slavery. However, for our purposes here, we can assume a connection between them as we pursue the idea of freedom. In order to do this, it is necessary to digress as we describe the master/slave relationship and how it represents the concepts of inequality and equality.

Master and Slave

In the book *Freedom*, slavery is defined as "the permanent, violent, and personal domination of natally alienated and generally dishonored persons." This relationship between master and slave is about as unequal as it gets, according to the definition. Domination of the slave, often by violence or coercion, is a major part of an extreme and unequal relationship. In addition, the slave is considered "socially dead" and does not belong to the legitimate social or moral community.

The master and his group are described as "parasitically gain(ing) honor in degrading the slave." Throughout both of these books are numerous descriptions of the master's personality being changed by the relationship with his slaves. References to masters being more authoritarian, being more inclined to obey their superiors, having greater skepticism about religious matters, engaging in more sexual exploitation of slave women, and having a general contempt for manual labor were all mentioned. These characteristics were attributed not only specifically to the master, but also to all authoritarian types.

This personality of the master seemed to describe a kind of aristocratic personality that provided a role model for future authoritarian governances throughout the development of western civilization. Although, throughout history, aggressive leaders prevailed over groups of people everywhere, it was not until the fully developed stereotype of the master appeared, along with the written word, that organized tyrants of many stripes were given full reign. These tyrants loosed the fires of a kind of aggressive empiricism together with technological progress that has been unparalleled in human history. Yet this system, for all its harm, was the beginning of scientific thought, individualism, and material benefits beyond belief.

The slave himself was portrayed as isolated, alienated, exploited, and totally dominated by the master. The master could only justify his existence by his perception of dominance over his slave. Part of that perception consisted of the master envisioning himself as having the very freedom about which the slave could only dream. The master was only free to the extent that he could compare himself with his slaves' lack of freedom. It was inferred that the slave did feel more secure and protected as a result of his relationship with his master.

There was little reference throughout Dr. Patterson's book to the personality of the slave as it focused mostly on his condition. In fact, throughout both books, the emphasis was on the slave's condition. The actual relationship between master and slave, as well as the slave himself, was left unclear.

It was a generalization that was offered in *Slavery and Social Death* (Patterson, 1982) that seemed to offer some explanation regarding why cultures in antiquity could not value personal freedom or equality as we know it. It was said that "premodern . . . non-slaveholding . . . societies . . . could not, value the removal of (societal) restraint . . . (because) . . . they yearned only for the security of being positively anchored in a network of power and authority . . . happiness was membership; being was belonging." This was not freedom, as we know it.

It may be that nature itself seemed so threatening to unorganized prehistoric individuals that it intimidated them. It also appears that security and protection experienced in premodern societies are similar to the security and protection that the slave experienced from the relationship with his master. After all, structure does provide protection and a feeling of security, even today. The Romans offered "bread and circuses," a patronage system and lower taxes in return for respect that, in turn, gave the free Romans the feeling of security and protection.

Apparently, the beginning of slavery, and particularly the Roman idea of manumission, gave rise to the idea of freedom through the living unspoken example of the master–slave relationship in their midst. That graphic example chillingly gave slow rise to an awareness of what happens when other people, instead of nature, impose absolute constraints on people or an individual. Apparently, it also slowly gave rise to the opposite desire to eliminate these same constraints.

Interdependency

Dr. Patterson (1991) describes three types of freedom in his book. However, personal freedom was only a flight of fancy until the eighteenth century when western civilization began implementing the idea. Remember, sovereign freedom traditionally has been reserved for emperors, kings, gentleman aristocrats, and authorities in general, while the average citizen or tribe member had little to none. The idea was for the sovereign to be made free in order to give good things back to his subjects. The sovereign lived with a god-like aura or illusion given to him by his subjects that could be likened to a cultural delusion or illusion. There were no opposing points of view to confuse the issue. In addition, because the sovereign was free, he was also easily corrupted because of a lack of constraints.

Civic freedom, then, was a special privilege obtained by a responsible citizen following the law. The citizens of the ancient Greek/Roman world, who fought wars valiantly for freedom, were fighting for sovereign and civic freedoms. Those people fighting those wars appreciated the improved standard of living and protection provided by sovereign and civic freedoms.

Personal freedom, particularly in America, was thought of as a lack of constraint for practically everything. That thought, according to Dr. Francis Fukuyama in his book *The End of History and the Last Man* (1992), has brought about and fostered "a combination of civic participation and organized polities" that are unique to democracies.

In other words, freeing citizens from certain shackles obtained more community participation. That was true particularly in politics, government, and community, utilizing counter-veiling power instead of absolute power. Apparently, when Americans adopted the ideals of personal freedom and equality, the protection and security offered by tyrants, despots, or benevolent dictators was partially diminished. In order to regain those feelings, more community participation became necessary.

One can imagine that an emphasis on personal freedom may conflict with the more traditional sovereign and civic freedoms as they all interact together. Such an emphasis could shatter any illusions that people have about the benevolence of sovereigns. In other words, it could result in dislike of authority and/or disrespect for law. It could also result in more anxiety and alienation for the people, since lack of constraints can reduce the security and protection provided by sovereign and law.

As one sheds the shackles of domination, it is the premise of this book that government or society is weakened. Remember, under authoritarian governance, absolute power is meted out by organizing activities designed to provide protection and the feeling of security to its citizens or tribe members. It is also true that any unequal vertical organization imposed on those same people by absolute authority is another kind of extended control or constraint. When the constraints are lifted for the persecuted, the constraints that bind many vertical hierarchies are also affected.

KINDS OF FREEDOM AND EQUALITY BY GOVERNMENT

Kind of Government	Kind of Freedom	Inequality or equality
Authoritarian	*Sovereign and Civic*	*Inequality*
Democracy	*Personal or Popular*	*Equality*

Table 1

As can be seen from Table 1, democracies, particularly one striving for an ideal democracy, must purge itself of any vestiges of authoritarian controls. These controls are derived from sovereign and civic freedoms and involve many inequalities. A democracy, on the other hand, advocates personal freedom in tandem with equality. A democracy, with all that freedom, may also distort the true meaning of personal freedom. It appears that both the simple popular view and the official personal view of freedom have an unhealthy emphasis on the removal of constraints.

A pure democratic state can only be achieved by following the tenets of personal freedom and equality without any reference to authoritarianism. Yet it is equally clear that one cannot exist without the other, since democracy evolves from authoritarianism and remains dependent on it. From now on, when referring to personal or popular freedom, it will be assumed that we are referring to a lack of constraints as the primary part of the definition.

The focus of this chapter has been on the evolution of freedom, including the conflicts between the old and new kinds. The rapid development of personal and popular freedoms in the last few centuries in our modern democracies has accompanied a rapid increase in concern for equality. The problem with these developments is that unevaluated harm is also present. The next chapter discusses in more detail on what is meant by equality.

3

Equality

> Democracy full of variety and disorder, and dispensing a sort of
> equality to equals and unequals alike.

—Plato

Freedom and equality are the motivating forces behind the whole of western civilization. It is the spirit of the enlightenment, the industrial revolution, the protestant revolution, and modern science. For many centuries, these movements have been gaining speed using technological innovation as the means to progress. The popular ideas heralding the progressive movement of the twentieth century were freedom and equality. The idea of progress has been linear, with no thought of human ideas being cyclical.

Our popular and somewhat simplistic ideas of freedom have come to be defined primarily as the condition of being free of constraints. After browsing the Internet for a definition of equality, it became clear that the word is "a loaded and highly contested concept . . . that has a rhetorical power rendering it suitable as a political slogan" (*Stanford Encyclopedia of Philosophy*, 2007 revision).

For the purpose of this book, equality will mean the quality or condition of being the same, in whole or in part. It seems, looking at our definitions, that equality is a difficult, often political term meaning the condition of being the same. Freedom and equality together suggest the imposition of sameness on a condition of being free of constraints. That is, each individual who is free must have the same amount of freedom. Without that kind of sameness of freedom, we have the condition of inequality where coercion and corruption of individuals by others can happen.

In practical politics, equality operates in tandem with freedom. That partnership is necessary because freedom alone produces conflict, chaos, and anarchy. Cultural deterioration is produced as people demand freedom from the rules and laws in any culture. The spirit of popular freedom demands the lessening of cultural constraints, even if they are essential.

The idea of equality, superimposed over individual freedom, limits each individual at the point where individual freedom is harmful to others. It serves to check and constrain individual freedom so that structural disorganization is minimized. Legal equality, then, defines the boundaries of freedom for each individual or group. In this way, legal equality insures equal freedom for all while containing cultural conflicts. If some were unequal, the difference would allow individual coercion, elitism, and intimidation to develop.

The War Against Inequality

Before the enlightenment, the idea of freedom was much different. The difference was mainly that sovereign and civic freedoms were unequal, as it depended on honor, status, and money. The inequalities inherent in these freedoms were accepted as part of that kind of freedom. Years after the enlightenment, encouraged by the words of Friedrich Nietzsche, personal freedom became a movement against tyrants, rigid unfair laws, and injustice in general.

Science was the motor of this spirit, the *Zeitgeist*, as technological innovation in the industrial revolution moved us away from dependence on slaves, dictators, and overly rigid laws. Personal freedom and equality developed together with this emerging new age. The *Zeitgeist* was a government by the people, free from tyranny, and meant equality for all.

The new idea of freedom evolved within the new emerging democracies as the older ideas of freedom were reduced or eliminated. Of course, the older ideas were housed within organized hierarchies that were based on inequalities. The new personal freedom demanded equality through networking and peer groups. Equality, then, was publically thought to be in conflict with inequalities in our modern culture. Yet it is equally clear that, in reality, each is fundamentally dependent on each other.

In fact, today science, government, religion, military, and others are all part of the old inequalities. Each institution requires constraint, discipline, and inequality. In the recent past, when our society loosened constraints and imposed equality, tremendous benefits and prosperity followed initially. That prosperity was attributed to personal freedom and equality. It was the motivating spirit of the times; it was our new *Zeitgeist*.

Economic freedom in the form of free enterprise has produced enormous prosperity. In the cultural sphere, more recently, social freedom has developed in the form of a series of social issues designed to free the oppressed. Social freedom is also expected to produce more prosperity. In each area, prosperity is expected but the harm of freedom is not discussed. The more cultural constraints we remove, the more individuals feel anxious, uncertain, and alienated. A world without structure is very upsetting indeed.

Inequality is the host that thrives on hierarchies. It is my thought that there is an unspoken war going on in America today between personal freedom and equality and the other two types of freedom that rely on inequality. This war is interwoven with cultural biases that make it impossible for Americans or anyone else to actually see and address the problem. The problem is too basic. Equality and inequality are engaging in a secret war when they should be complimenting each other.

The Roots of Inequality

In order to fully understand how this war is affecting all of us, we must consider inequality and its roots in slavery in more detail. The most unequal human relationship one can think of is the master–slave relationship. In modern terms, that means a predator–victim relationship. In Fukuyama's book, *The End of History and the Last Man*, the master–slave relationship is portrayed in depth as he discusses the possible origins of authoritarian and democratic forms of government. He says the following, as he paraphrases Hegel:

> "According to Hegel, the desire for recognition initially drives two primordial combatants (master and slave) to seek to make the other recognize their humanness by staking their lives in a mortal battle. When the natural fear of death leads one combatant to submit, the relationship of master and slave is born."

Fukuyama goes on to describe this primitive battle as one of pure virtues like prestige and honor as the combatants seek personal recognition and self-esteem by the total exploitation and/or domination of the other. We see this often in our modern world, as people in conflict seek total control over others in failed personal relationships. For groups in conflict, the ideal is war; for individuals in conflict, the ideal is murder.

The relationship of lordship and bondage (master–slave) inherent in most ancient organized groups of people was then "overcome as a result of the French and . . . American revolutions" (Fukuyama, 1992). The inference here seems to be that the recent pursuit of personal freedom has upended the centuries-old reign of the master as creator of the authoritarian way of government and its unequal freedoms. Implicit in this relationship is something very basic to human nature: the need to dominate others as well as to control nature itself. We can see evidence of this need to dominate everywhere in our society where success is often rewarded far beyond reason. On the fringes, unlawful predatory behavior is increasingly prevalent as crime increases.

Strangely enough, even the predator–victim relationship has its benefits and harm. Even science itself, as it seeks to harness nature, has benefits and harm. The harm is symbolized in our modern science fiction movies in which mad scientists are creating monsters or trying to take over the world. The harm must be symbolized because most people consciously see only scientific benefits. Likewise, the predator–victim relationship has benefits as the teacher–student and policeman–criminal relationships use assertive mild intimidation as controls to nurture learning, responsible citizenship, and responsible control and punishment of criminals.

There was an inference in Fukuyama's book that the master part of the master–slave relationship is strongly associated with the tendency throughout history to engage in war and empire building. Conversely, the slave part is anti-war and anti-expansionistic since the slave mentality is one of the victims yearning to be free. He goes on to describe this radical relationship as one that cannot be analyzed without including other unequal relationships that are far less dominating. What he refers to are all other vertical or hierarchical relationships in society.

The difference between these other relationships and the master–slave is "the relative power of the master . . . where . . . power is usually confined to a specific range of activities." There was even mention of the modern relation between baseball players and owners in our democracy where they are impersonally traded by owners, as if they were, in part, slaves. These other unequal relationships only included partial power over the lesser person and oftentimes were beneficial to society or individuals. In all cases of vertical relationships, control is involved to some degree. A discussion like this is a clear reminder that there is no society that is purely democratic or authoritarian. Today in America, we are a bit of both. However, it is clear to me that American freedom and its equality are in direct conflict with controls and constraints that are necessary.

All of these vertical relationships echo the sentiment of the original first recorded human organization where a physically strong leader required submission through conflict in order to lead and protect the less physically strong group members. The master–slave relationship was radical in that—the power of the master over the slave was absolute. The requirement of one group or individuals' submission under another is an old idea that stands at the core of the authoritarian idea. While this is an ultimate in unequal relations, equality of relationships poses another no less important problem.

The master's absolute control over the slave as well as the other lesser unequal relationships apparently provided secondary gain to citizens as protection and security. As a result of the existence of that radical relationship and the use of manumission to free the slaves, masters and slaves could see firsthand experience of what it was like to dominate and restrict other human beings totally. That awareness, over time, allowed for the development of an enhanced awareness of what it meant to be a slave, a master, or both.

Both Dr. Patterson and Fukuyama focused on the slave and his yearning for freedom in their books. However, Fukuyama went on to describe the needs and desires in the master, which evolved into modern authoritarianism and totalitarianism that "sought (often) to control all aspects of human life." As I understand it, the master symbolized authoritarian governance and the slave represented democratic governance. We now need to discuss how the dominating master part of the master–slave relationship represented a way of governing, just as the dominated slave represented a more recent way of governing and living.

But don't be fooled for a moment. The harm inherent in either of these forms of governance *alone* is ominous; only the two operating in tandem can produce a workable, effective, and satisfying society. A thorough understanding of authoritarian and democratic structures is important now, but the idea of several kinds of freedom coexisting is our primary concern.

The relationships between the different kinds of freedom need be explored extensively in order to determine how these entities can best operate together. The most grievous problem in the past has been the view that masters and slaves are separate. The introduction of the idea of a relationship between them conjures up the idea that they depend upon one another to some extent.

Aside from the benefits of sovereign freedom, when the Greeks and Romans added law as part of governance, people felt even more secure under the newly added civic freedom. They felt secure as long as they were law abiding, and the laws were strictly enforced. It was a privilege to be a citizen in a civilization based on glaring inequalities. In those days, nature often intimidated people, forcing them to organize themselves. There were also other organized groups of enemies, sometimes called barbarians, which threatened these organized groups. However, with sovereign freedom came the inequality of vertical hierarchies, which was the most efficient way of organizing groups.

These vertical hierarchies were absolutely necessary for the efficient operation of the government regardless of kind. In fact, vertical hierarchies are still important, even to modern democracies. In the old days, the person at the top, the sovereign, had full freedom, and, as you go down the hierarchy, people had less and less freedom.

The people had constraints imposed with the understanding that they would reap benefits. Sovereign constraints were communicated to them as edicts from the ultimate authority. Communication in those days consisted in large part of direct orders or accusations as a way to enforce the vertical hierarchy. Civic constraints also required using the same kind of communication in order to enforce the law. There seemed to be little awareness of interpersonal communication in order to better know each other as equals that we know today.

In modern authoritarian systems, inequalities continue to abound. In modern democratic governments, particularly in America, there appears to be a knee-jerk reaction to eliminate most of the inequalities that still exist. This means sovereign and civil freedoms are adversely affected. The American civil rights movement in its modern expanded form seems to be implementing equality everywhere without any concern for the consequences.

Equality even seems to be so entrenched that it is actually considered to be a legitimate part of logic. Seemingly reasonable people argue that "so and so did it" as if the fact that someone else engaged in a certain behavior is reason enough for them to engage in it themselves. Whatever "they" did is all right for "them" to do, since they are all equal. Another thing about the logic of equality is that the term "fair" has come to be interchangeable with the word "equal." If one argues the fairness of something, they are arguing really for equality. The truth is that many things are not equal, and logic cannot easily apply equality to situations that are grossly different.

The relationship with the master creates a yearning for freedom within the slave, but it also creates resentment. Without that relationship with the master, neither yearning nor resentment would occur. So it follows that the ideas of personal freedom and equality, as conceived by the slave, are dependent on the very ideas he is trying to eliminate. As the saying goes, no man (or idea) is an island.

This analysis of freedom and equality clearly describes its mindless acceptance throughout the western world. The general public and politicians do not seem to have any real modern understanding of America and its freedoms. Instead, we have constant tumult where, eventually out of disgust, progress is cited as the cure. The progress is depicted over and over as technological innovation as new benefits are touted. Nowhere is any harm considered a part of progress.

Americans are not cognizant of the fact that science and logic are derived from authoritarianism's inequalities. In education, the din of critique about unfair treatment of students moves us ever closer to full equality for all. Even government has pressures to shed itself of its elitist posturing and its corrupt patronage system. In the criminal justice system, the decriminalization of the system is a blatant attempt to equalize the system to its criminals. One example might be the granting of equal rights to terrorists, which has the potential to catapult them into the ranks of victims of the U.S. military.

Because hierarchies of all kinds in the external world are under pressure to become more equal, organizing activities itself is being weakened. Furthermore, since traditional reasoning still prevails in the face of a new kind of modern reasoning, science, politicians, and the general populace are exhibiting poorer judgment. The result is not a populace that is more uniform, fair, or equal. Instead, it seems that a general rage is erupting against anonymous authority.

The endpoint of this diatribe is to depict western civilization as an entity that assures both equality and inequality for all. It is now thought to bring only prosperity and happiness with no mention of any of the problems associated with it. What is clear is that this rough-hewn equality depends exclusively on distrust of all authority, law, and unequal hierarchies. There is an invisible internal war being waged in America and, it is between equality and inequality.

4

Constraints

> Personal freedom . . . is not being coerced or restrained by
> another person.
> —Orlando Patterson

Theoretically, a slave freed into an environment with no constraints, would not know what to do. That freed person would have no inner resources like self-discipline, conscience, or experience, and no external constraints like rewards and punishments to serve as a guide for responsible action. The proponents of personal freedom and equality theorize that full equality and open communication conjoint with no external constraints are the ideal to which our secular society is moving. A person in a structureless external world, not guided by internal values and with no experience, is held up as an ideal circumstance.

To me, this existential condition is a springboard for feelings of insecurity, of being alone, and more chaos and anarchy. As the security and protection provided by what is left of the old system is further dismantled, cultural harms such as crime, mental illness, and cultural deterioration follow. Keeping this secular ideal and its consequences in mind, it is important now to clarify what is meant by constraint, restraint, and structure.

Definitions

In this narrative, constrain means to restrain by force or confine *(Collins English Dictionary,* 2003). The word "restrain" is similar, as its popular meaning is to hold back or keep in check. In one instance, restrain was

33

defined as a rule or condition that limits freedom *(English Dictionary, World Reference.com,* 2008). In general, the words "restrain" and "constrain" are interchangeable, except the word "constrain" is used more often when force is involved. In this narrative, the only inappropriate use of "restrain" and "constrain" will be some of the official quotes of other authors.

The word "structure" is another matter. The common meaning of the word is that it is a complex system considered from the point of view of the whole. In this book, however, its use is more psychosocial. By that I mean structure often also provides protection and security to those who dwell within it. In this sense, the elimination of structure can produce a dysfunctional system as well as dysfunctional individuals. When the word "structure" is used in this monologue, it is considered to be a complex physical and mental system considered from the point of view of the whole, which provides protection and security to those who depend on it.

Control

Clearly, the idea of constraints centers around limiting individuals and groups. In this book, the limitations refer to confining behavior or ideas, which reduce one's freedom. The environment surrounding the individual or group is the arena in which the constraints are applied. That environment contains an almost infinite variety of ways to constrain behavior or thoughts. Law, policies, procedures, and edicts are some of the direct formal means to constrain, while tradition, mores, intimidation, manipulation, and competition are only a few of the indirect informal ways to constrain. Oftentimes, the application of constraints means controlling individuals or groups. Constraint of human behavior has been present throughout history in the form of control, particularly in authoritarian government. In democracies, control is more indirect, while the direct constraints are often viewed as harmful.

It is important to note that in both types of governing, control through the use of constraint is necessary in holding the system together. Initially, in ancient Greece and Rome, sovereign and civic freedoms were dependent on the control exercised by the sovereign and his laws. As a result, through the centuries, humans increasingly organized and controlled the population by defining specialists, inventing job descriptions, dividing labor, and creating numerous working parts for civilization.

The most direct primitive control, even in modern times, remains direct edicts and intimidation. More indirect coercive manipulations are another way to maintain control in a modern society. At the same time, maintenance of controls offered freedoms to citizens who were obedient within the hierarchy.

If the sovereign and his aristocrats could not maintain control, the people either rebelled or the sovereign organized against an outside enemy to re-achieve control. The point is that control has always been necessary but so has its opposite freedom. The kind of freedom that comes with constraints, however, is a different kind of freedom. It is freedom within hierarchies; it is unequal freedom and it is compatible with absolute authority and law. It has the feel of being protected and secure as if in the womb. It is not the kind of freedom most Americans seek today.

Control seems to work best in the realm of the inanimate because inanimate objects behave consistently, are viewed as separate and distinct from one another, do not feel pain as control is imposed, and behave predictably under controlled conditions. They are measurable and predictable and are, therefore, easily controlled. Although it is necessary to maintain control over humans within the controlling system, it is a much more difficult and subtle thing to administer.

This battle between master and slave describes the very core of what it means to be human as it shows clearly man's need for control over other humans as well as nature. In fact, even today, this primordial battle continues as many authoritarian and totalitarian governances joust for absolute control. Even in democracies that abhor the tyrant, control is necessary. In democracies, the control is more indirect by manipulation, mild intimidation, or competition.

Who among you has not noticed the harm caused by someone who tries to control everyone? According to the tenets of the master–slave ideology, this attempt to control other humans is a basic human trait. When it is done with harm in mind, it hurts people; when it is done with benefits in mind, it helps people. The point is that beneficial control is needed but generally control is viewed as totally harmful in modern America.

Americans have a history of dislike for absolute authority and aristocrats. However, they utilize the same methods of organizing and thinking that is considered authoritarian. We use the same science, technology, and many of the same traditions. Our pluralistic democracy is basically democratic ideas superimposed upon an authoritarian base. The democratic ideas include equal freedom for all with no constraints. That translates into the ideal of no control at all. No control at all is also called personal or the simplified popular version called popular freedom.

America, in its quest for equal freedom for all, uses equality as a catalyst for organized control as personal and popular freedoms eliminate or reduce constraints. These constraints are, more or less, associated with traditional controls on behavior. Equality is a stabilizing influence over the disorganization that can result from loosened constraints. It is a kind of organized control that works best under stress. It reinforces equality of treatment between individuals and groups so they do not harm each other. At the same time, equality punishes restricting constraints by condemning them as unequal. In other words, the equality argument is that the traditional notion of inequality constricts and limits personal and popular freedoms.

It should be noted that there are different consequences for the two general types of government. Any authoritarian system in a crisis is likely to overcontrol its population in an attempt to reestablish control. Most of the time, these attempts result in a rigid, static, repressive situation that can result in anarchy or war. Democracies, on the other hand, have a history of loosening controls over time. The result over time is that a crisis is produced in the name of personal freedom. That crisis is the opposite of rigidity, as people become less able to discern differences between things. The result is something I call blurring, which involves a diminished clarity of the external world.

Democracies have a tendency to become disorganized under stress, as too many constraints are loosened. If control cannot be maintained, a blurring occurs that can result in rebellion and anarchy. If that blurring intensifies, then at the point of mass delusion, total anarchy conjoint with a primitive regression to rigid authoritarianism can be the result.

The gist of this narrative is that constraints are quite necessary in a democracy because it is necessary for our leaders to control the system in whatever way they can. In crisis, that control is even more necessary. All national states in crisis experience the possibility of regressing back to a more primitive predator–victim relationship.

However, democratic systems experience blurring first, then there is a danger of a belated regression to a rigid sovereign. In an authoritarian system, rigidity and repressive overcontrol occur first; unless that system attacks an external enemy. The point here is that control is necessary no matter whether rigidity or blurring is present. The concept of blurring will be discussed later in another section.

Consequences

It is clear at this point that constraints in the service of control are quite necessary for efficient governing. It is also evident that the pursuit of personal or popular freedom *alone* is inadequate, since it advocates a lack of constraint along with equality. Such a pursuit inevitably results in the weakening of controls throughout our culture, particularly those that involve unequal traditional hierarchies. What is not clear are the consequences that are now present that are harmful to us.

The resurfacing of past-suppressed conflicts when governmental or cultural structure is suddenly absent or ineffective is a modern Pandora's Box. In other words, the lifting of constraints conjoint with the application of equality can cause age-old cultural conflicts to erupt. An easy example of this resurfacing of an age-old problem is the ethnic cleansing that occurred in Bosnia after the Soviet Union, a now defunct totalitarian government, suddenly relinquished its hold on eastern European countries.

When the accepted absolute distinctions and boundaries set down in a ruthless manner under the Soviet Union were abandoned, age-old ethnic conflicts surfaced and war erupted in some places. In addition, the war in Iraq was a shock to the American psyche when old conflicts between Muslim sects erupted when we destroyed the old structure of Saddam Hussein. The shock, to Americans, was that they had no idea that those suppressed ethnic conflicts would erupt with the lifting of constraints. If Americans had been cognizant of the consequences of forcibly removing controls through war with Iraq, those ancient conflicts may not have happened.

It should be considered that all these events are happening because constraints have been lifted and old clear distinctions between things are diminishing. That diminishment is occurring because of two things: 1) the application of equality to the unequal and 2) a general blurring of boundaries associated with removal of constraints. Both of these reasons also contribute to the current malaise in America and the anonymous cultural harm that has been occurring.

It is clear to me that rewards and punishment by most societies are the means by which law is enforced. Using social engineering as a way to influence the populace, governments the world over have rewarded their citizens for good behavior and punished them for bad behavior. Governmental leaders and aristocrats of many kinds in the past have managed their citizens without much publicity regarding their methods. Status, recognition, and money have generally served as rewards, while our prisons, jails, intimidation, and coercion have served as punishment.

Some groups suffer veiled harm that is generally unspeakable while other groups experience benefits. The public is clearly aware of the benefits as America prospers. The public is partially aware of the harm to the extent that it harms certain minority groups. However, most Americans have no awareness that cultural harm is associated with our ideas of freedom. The result is a lack of concern for increased crime rates, divorces, and mental illness. In the next section, some statistical data is offered that documents much of that harm.

The Harm of Freedom

In Fukuyama's book, *The Great Disruption* (1999), statistical data was presented that indicates huge harmful cultural changes erupting from the early 1960s to the present time. All of the described countries were democratic and technologically sophisticated. He portrayed these changes as an adaptation to the coming information age. The violent crime line graph (Graph 1) depicts a huge increase in violent crimes in the early 1960s. The one exception is Japan.

Fukuyama explained in his book that the decriminalization movement of the 1970s and 1980s most likely was associated with the great disruption in America. He argues that the court rulings regarding decriminalization were based on the reasoning "that certain criminal sanctions violated the rights of individuals to free speech, due process and the like."

Also, in the theft crime graph (Graph 2), that same mid-century upsurge occurs in every country again, except Japan. It is tempting to think that crime in most developed nations generally varies with the number and kind of cultural constraints. It is possible to imagine that the idea of freedom and equality became so dominant in the early 1960s that constraints were loosened, and harm resulted in the form of a great cultural disruption.

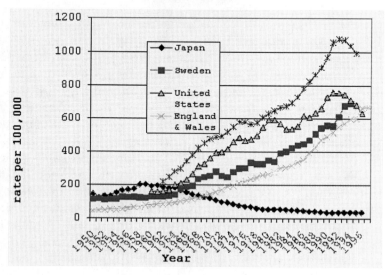

Graph 1

Source: See Appendix.

Both Graph 1 and 2 indicate that many developed democracies experienced that same cultural disruption. The disruptions of violent and property crime together at the same time on the graphs suggest that the change is general throughout the technologically developed democratic world. This data is suggestive enough that a general basic concept like freedom and equality may ultimately help explain this.

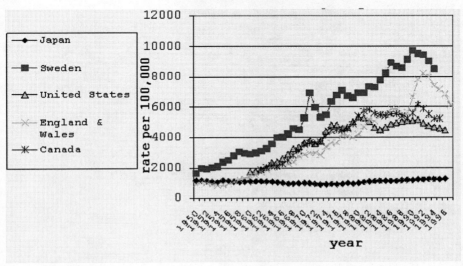

Graph 2

Source: See Appendix.

The last graph (Graph 3) compares divorce rates over time for the same developed countries. In this graph, the same abrupt increases occur, but this time, America is way ahead in the number of divorces. As Francis Fukuyama said, "the great disruption was characterized by increasing levels of crime and social disorder, (including) the decline of families and kinship." He goes on to describe the early 1960s to the present time as "a striking pattern of growing disorder."

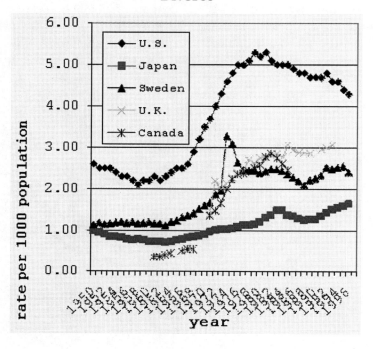

Graph 3

Source: See Appendix.

There were numerous other sets of statistical data presented in Fukuyama's book that reinforced the idea of a great disruption. Fukuyama made it clear the disruption was not specific to a single developed democratic country. He also suggested that the disruption is related to creative technological innovation as we move toward the new information age. In this book, while agreeing with him, the innovation introducing the new age is depicted as producing both benefits and harm. The harm is increasing social disorder and the decline of kinship described by Fukuyama. All of the aforementioned cultural deterioration is, in this author's opinion, associated with a widespread unarticulated view of freedom as a loosening of human constraints.

Fukuyama then went on to portray our culture as building a "very powerful . . . theme: that of the liberation of the individual from unnecessary and stifling social constraints." Lip service was also paid to freedom and equality when Fukuyama stated that "a society built around information tends to produce more . . . freedom and equality."

While constraints, to a point, may be beneficial, beyond a certain point, it may produce harm. At the point of crisis, discipline and control become more necessary. It may be that we are now at the point of crisis where creative thinking and disciplined acts are important. The point is that a mindless removing of constraints in the name of freedom is a bad idea. It appears that cultural change has its consequences: its benefits and harm. The expectation of great benefits for innovation and change is wrong unless the harm is also considered. The next chapter depicts an ancient regime that also may have had similar problems.

5

The Ides of March

A great civilization is not conquered from without until it has
destroyed itself from within.

—Will Durant

Amidst all this bantering about equal freedom for all and their effect on
various parts of American culture, scarcely little has been stated about one of
the oldest semi-democratic governments: the ancient Roman Republic. The
portrayal of the ancient Roman Republic will depict that regime as one that
adheres to certain kinds of freedom and no equality what so ever.

In order to cover the territory accurately and quickly, I will make reference
to the book *Rubicon* (2003) by Tom Holland. In that book, Holland covers the
spectacular development and abrupt demise of that republic. Of all the books
I have read on the subject, this one comes nearest to explaining in detail why
the republic imploded. What follows is a set of quotes that suggest why it
fell.

- "the roman people . . . in the end, grew tired of antique virtue."
- "Senators might prefer to tolerate any amount of low level anarchy
  (rather than to) grant to clear . . . (problems) . . . up."
- "the arts of persuasion were increasingly being abandoned to . . .
  (a) . . . resort . . . to violence and intimidation."
- "the fruit of too much liberty is slavery." (by Cicero)

It was stated in the book that the republic had partial free speech, private
property, some liberty, and rights before the law. Perhaps, the most glaring
difference that I noticed was how politics and military were intertwined.

Burnt Offerings   43

There were apparently no distinctions made between the two, as political and military responsibilities seemed one and the same. In addition, there was no law enforcement as we know it, but they did have courts that passed down punishment.

A frequent result of not having a police force meant that lots of people were exiled. The republic did have written laws but the law was considered an extension of politics and was conducted in private. The result of having a newly organized political system meant that not much specialization occurred.

The same was true of the fabled engineering feats of the Romans, since they too were extensions of politics. Although they had some freedom, there was no equality. Inequality was strongly associated with their sense of community. As living proof of inequality, they had a thriving slave population. It was a highly stratified society where both women and slaves were not Roman citizens. Even among the citizens, envy and malice produced high status for those with money and a good family background. That, however, was perilous status . . ."only if it inspired fear without undue resentment." The point is that the republic's checks and balances controlled each Roman's native sense of glory and channeled it into a ferocious competitiveness. It is my thought that the ambition and greed of most people in the republic was what fueled the republic. Their lives were spent seeking after glory, in competition with other glory-seekers.

From the very beginning, the ancient customs and laws were inculcated into each citizen to ensure that "never again should one man be permitted to rule supreme in Rome." Those ancient customs and laws included the virtues of courage, strength, ability, excellence, piety, and fidelity. According to the book, the children of the republic were almost never described as dependents and were treated sternly with little show of emotion. As adults, these same people were fiercely competitive, particularly the males. The republic itself controlled and constrained each citizen, while granting them some freedom, as we know it. However, they had no equality, for "only slaves on the chain gang were equal."

In the later years, that competitive urge contained by law erupted when Caesar overthrew it and formed a monarchy. It was then that Caesar and his partisans, "freed of (the) restraints and inhibitions of tireless convention . . . (had) grown . . . intoxicated by a world in which . . . there were no limits." To our modern way of thinking, they were free. But make no mistake, there were times when the republic was still partially intact and the ancient values were still imagined. The senators or other influential citizens could have had the old regime reinstated, but they declined. They were apparently tired of all the senatorial bickering and constant war. So as the Romans themselves recognized, "their freedom contained the seeds of its own ruin."

The ancient values of glory, strength, and honor encumbered by the republican checks and balances, which worked so well for almost half a millennium, were no more. The end finally came in 44 BC when over seventy senators overcame Caesar and killed him in an act of retribution. Caesar ignored warnings from friends and a soothsayer to beware the Ides of March, for his life was in danger. The politicians involved in plotting and implementing Caesar's death thought it would bring back the republic, but instead it made Caesar a martyr.

From this brief synopsis of the Roman Republic, two obvious cultural traits differentiate the Roman culture from our current brand of western culture. The first and most obvious is the lack of equality. The second is the intense public political conflicts that led to the republic's demise.

The Romans had a highly stratified society in which neither women nor slaves were citizens. Among the citizens, there was an ongoing group of political elitists at the top of a vertical hierarchy. In order to be a member of the elite, one came from an aristocratic family that owned property and/or had money. The rest of the citizens, apparently, were allowed a better standard of living, relative freedom of speech, and some rights as citizens as long as they followed the law. They were, on occasion, given food and circuses for being good citizens. Roman citizens were proud of their limited freedom, but equality was never considered.

Another glaring difference was the intense internal and external conflicts, which were public issues, particularly near the end. The entire book portrayed the Romans in one lethal conflict after another, until the republic failed and a monarchy rose in its stead. The republic itself was an attempt to socialize conflicts, and its solution was to superimpose law and politics on the Roman people. By institutionalizing ritual as law and politics, they also made the conflicts public as they allowed some free speech. However, the vast majority of Roman subjects were illiterate, superstitious, and intensely emotional. They knew little else but inequality in its extreme: a master–slave relationship or something closer.

As I finished reading this book, I had the distinct feeling that the common men of the Roman Empire were closer to cavemen than we are today. Like cavemen, they had few productive leisure activities to vent their thoughts and emotions. Language and writing were new and, apparently, their thoughts and emotions were expressed rather bluntly and absolutely. The result seems to have been a plethora of interpersonal tragedies as they tried to use language and writing to build a cooperative society. As a result, they may have been less ready for the freedom they acquired than we have been. One might think that they had a thin veneer of republican government encumbering a rather primitive uncivil populace.

You must remember that these brutes were private, unsophisticated people with access to few or no technology for communication, traveling, or even thinking. In addition, they didn't seem to play much. From my reading, they appeared to be virtually trapped within themselves with few external outlets. The world may have appeared as a new plaything, but they had access to few toys. The result, to my way of thinking, is that they appeared to be rather rigid absolute traditional types.

These people sought solace in the attainment of elite status in their new society in the attainment of predator warrior/political status through primitive competition with barbarian nation/tribes or by interaction between fellow Romans for honor and glory. In the beginning, the imposition of law and free speech on such people must have been a highly unpredictable balance. Still, since it lasted almost 500 years, it was unbelievably successful.

The Romans of that time, like Americans, may well have initially seen only the benefits of a republic, with the harm only developing later. In their case, the harm seemed to take the form of intense conflicts erupting that were contained for long period of time, but the compromises were often examples of poor judgment. Apparently, in the end, that indecision or poor judgment resulted in apathy and hostility, which prevented the Romans from reinstating the republic. Perhaps, they preferred the protection and security of a monarchy to the trials and tribulations of the republic.

It was also clear to me, from reading *Rubicon* that only limited sovereign and civil freedoms were involved in the republic. When the monarchy replaced it, the sovereign and civic freedoms continued in large part. The change seemed to be that the senate no longer had any power and in its place was the emperor. The conflicts between senators were gone, together with the freedom to disagree between senators. Since both the republic and the emperor gave their citizens limited sovereign and civic freedoms, all that they seemed to lose in the transition is the constant public bickering and indecisiveness in the senate.

The reasons for the demise of Rome long ago are still debated in our time, but my thought is that they lost very little in becoming a monarchy. Then, as today, the idea of containing and resolving human problems by using opposing extremes in government was alive. Opposing points of view in conflict were active then, as they are today. Those conflicts were resolved fairly effectively for 500 years using government and politics as arbiter.

Today, our resources are more abundant for problem solving but regression back to the primitive master–slave relationship remains a possible option. External war then, as now, was and is the ultimate method of creating internal unity in a badly divided republic or democracy.

It does appear that American democracy has much more ability to socially contain problems and resolve them than the old Roman Republic. The complete lack of formal personal freedom or equality made the Romans quite different from modern Americans. Our evolution of an organized division of labor and specialization that has resulted in a tremendous technological revolution also illustrates how very different we are from the Romans.

Yet one cannot help but see similarities between our current corrupt politicians and their continual bickering and the Roman senate's corruptness. It is interesting to theorize that modern American politics are similar in some ways to the old Roman Republic. The words of John Adams ring true when he wrote in 1814 in a letter to John Taylor, "Remember democracy never lasts long. It soon wastes, exhausts, and murders itself."

Although there is little information available today about whether the ancient regime's senate had any external constraints at all, it does seem plausible that there were few to none. If so, it can be theorized that the lack eventually produced stalemate, rigid polarization, and corruption much like American politics today.

Yet our democracy is completely different in that it pursues personal freedom and equality instead of sovereign and civic freedoms and inequality. It also has well-organized and well-developed technology that is highly specialized. As a result, our culture is able to sustain unheard-of technological innovation, including communication technology. However, it seems that politics and government have lagged far behind in the American technological revolution and have exhibited poor problem-solving ability and corruption for some time. Politics and government, with its old-time patronage system of special interests, appears similar in some ways to the ancient republic.

6

Examples

Example is the school of mankind, and they will learn at no other.
—Edmund Burke

Up to this point, what is meant by general constraints and structure have been covered. The idea of loosening constraints has been presented as having not only benefits, but also harm. More importantly, the concept of equality, that is associated with personal freedom, also produces harm. Neither concept has been thought to produce harm in the past. In fact, American freedom and equality are thought to be produced by technological progress, which is only beneficial. We have not spent time describing specific tangible examples of equality harming existing unequal hierarchies. This chapter is devoted to portraying several of these examples.

First, it is necessary to engage in a narrative about what is missing in the current information that the average American receives. For the most part, the media serves up a potpourri of singular events that can be harmful. For instance, suppose that a policeman engages in an illegal act against a citizen in the process of doing his job. There is no way for the average citizen to know how many other policemen conducted themselves honorably while doing that same job, since they frequently only rely on the media. The only way to get that kind of information is to be intimately involved with the criminal justice system.

Let me give you a clear example of a ratio giving us good information about an event that allows us to better understand the situation presented. When people produce automobiles, technology is required to carefully measure the product and its progress. Production has to be managed and controlled. Specific measurements need to be available to assure that the auto performs

48   Floyd Sours

correctly and consistently. The materials that are measured, for the most part, are inanimate, highly predictable, and consistent.

As for the people who drive the automobiles, measurement of their behavior as they drive automobiles is possible but more problematic because they are humans. As a greater number of people acquire automobiles, more benefits are documented. As time progresses, measurements begin to show accidents and injuries occurring documenting some harm as a by-product of the use of automobiles. It is a very useful and measurable system that yields excellent practical information about autos and their occupants.

According to the Office of Highway Policy Information within the Federal Highway Administration, in their Highway Statistics 2004, it is indicated that, in 2004, there were 43,636 fatalities in auto accidents compared to 226,621,674 licensed drivers. That works out to about 2/1000 of 1 percent deaths for all licensed drivers in the United States. This figure suggests a very low rate of harm compared to the benefits. Furthermore, since that number of fatalities has remained pretty much the same in recent years, the low harm ratio seems stable with no suggestion of significant change. Apparently, the system of producing, selling, and driving autos to the general public is alive and doing well. I submit that it is important to obtain that same data for any other organized system that produces change in order to really understand that system as it operates in our culture.

In the criminal justice system, our media present the harmful events of policemen, but give us no information about how many other policemen are doing their job in a beneficial way in that same system throughout the same time span. Unlike the case of the automobile, the data by the media about the police are woefully inadequate. We should be getting information about the benefits as well as the harm. Since we are not, we either draw untrue conclusions or none at all.

If we were to go a step further and try to compare the police with the criminals, we only know the harm of policemen and compare it to the perceived unfairness rendered to criminals. One example is the recent initiation of DNA testing for criminals that sometimes prove they are innocent. The public is never told how many people were found guilty who really were guilty. If you try to compare policemen to criminals using the media information, you might falsely conclude that policemen and law and order in general are worse than the criminals. It would be a case of comparing grossly dissimilar events to each other.

If the average person knew both the benefits and harm of any reported event, he would have a much better idea about how well the event is being managed. The current media method of disseminating information lacks the critical information one needs to make good judgments. In order to make good judgments on perceived harm, one must know both the harmful event and the general background of all such similar events. When that is obtained, it is possible to proceed with some reasonable conclusions. Where information on benefits and harm is missing, it is not possible to obtain clear conclusions.

Criminal Justice

Earlier, statistical data was presented that strongly suggested a spike in crime in the early 1960s. The data from Fukuyama's book, *The Great Disruption,* suggested that the disruption was associated with the decriminalization of the criminal justice system. While decriminalization through the courts was portrayed as a violation of individual rights for criminals, it is but one step to imagining that decriminalization is a legal move designed to eliminate constraints on criminals. In this section, practical examples will show how reducing constraints and applying equality can produce cultural weakening that taken altogether produces a great cultural disruption.

One example that has already been mentioned is the policeman and his formal relationship with the criminal. It is extremely important that the policemen continue to be unequal to the criminal in order to do his job effectively, just as the master must preserve his inequality to the slave. The current movement to decriminalize the criminal justice system has done great harm by unintentionally (and sometimes intentionally) making the policeman equal to the criminal.

The problem is that the average person sees the harmful events on television or the Internet, but cannot tell the difference between the harm created by police and the harm committed by the criminal. He also does not recognize that these events are significantly different from each other. He has not been given enough information for reasonable decision making. He is shown a specific example of harm for either the police or the criminal, but he is never shown the benefits and harm of each separate system.

He does know that harm has occurred but he does not have critical information about how frequently harm occurs in the system. The suggestion is that the harm committed by policemen and criminals is somehow comparable. As a result, there is an increasing inability to tell the difference between criminals and policemen in tandem with increased dysfunction in the criminal justice system.

The bias here is created by unavailability of data regarding people in the criminal justice system that is faithfully and legally doing their jobs. For the media, these unavailable tidbits are uninteresting and not newsworthy. On the other hand, the criminals who abuse the system are not well known either. For some reason, we only see the benefits to the criminal.

50 | Floyd Sours

An example would be when DNA evidence finds a convicted criminal innocent. In those cases, the media present the information in such a way that the criminal justice system is to be blamed. Yet it is the criminal justice system that began to use the DNA system in order to improve decision making. There is no data regarding how many criminals are actually guilty. There does not seem to be a fair balance between benefits and harm reported by the media. They seem to have some cultural bias against presenting both the policemen and the criminals.

This adds up to a rather skewed perception of the criminal justice system that lends itself to bad judgment by the general populace about the system. By allowing only partial information, the criminal justice system is incrementally undercut without any awareness of the public that it is happening. This kind of bias is enacted under the cover of equality, without any knowledge that the system is being damaged and the distribution of information is far from equal or fair. At a feeling level, most people have only a gnawing feeling that something is wrong, but they do not know why.

In the meantime, the decriminalization process reduces or, in some instances, entirely removes constraints on criminals. Decriminalization is a process that works to eliminate the stigma attached to being a criminal. This process is similar to the community mental health movement that is designed to remove the stigma of being a mental patient. By giving them more lenient conditions and reducing their punishment, constraints are reduced.

As a result, more criminals are abusing the law as they sue the courts and prisons regularly, communicate regularly outside prison, sometimes engage in crime in prison or jail, and have a plethora of pleasurable recreational and educational activities in prisons. In addition, more lenient sentences effectively reduce the effect of incarceration as punishment. These freedoms also have the effect of equalizing the distinction between responsible citizens, criminals, and illegal aliens. Then blurring occurs, and people can no longer distinguish differences easily between any of them.

Another example of needed inequalities in the same system is the distinction between guilt and innocence. Both Lowi's (1979) and Howard's (1994) books make reference to the increase in poor judgment in the court system and government. Apparently, the judges themselves have trouble determining guilt or innocence. That is because our culture has shifted its focus from the good of the community to whether bad behavior is fair and/or equal to other behaviors of its kind. In addition, increased emphasis on "due process" focuses on the process instead of the actual behavior being judged. The change of focus makes the judgment and the acquisition of justice ever more difficult.

This change of focus assures that the people in the system are now being trained to focus more on what is considered criminal behavior. We no longer are judging what is best for the community. All of this focus on process or the relativity of bad behavior is done in the name of more equality. They want everything in the process to be equal and fair. Our concern for justice is often lost in the process as we seek equality.

Imagine, if you can, a judge who personally cannot distinguish between important separate things, like good and bad. A judge like that is likely to be thought of as secular. Then, on top of that, all external constraints are removed. That is, many of the traditional laws, values, policies, or procedures that were designed to facilitate the judge's and the court's sovereignty, are gone, changed, or reduced.

You see, the judge did have sovereign freedom to make decisions. The advent of equality in the system means that he no longer can easily distinguish good from bad. Furthermore, the loosening or changing of constraints, particularly formal law, also makes justice through the courts an even harder task. As a result, no judgment can be made, and justice is not served. If the judge makes a forced judgment, not knowing the difference between good and bad, it would be just a guess, since he is lacking good judgment.

In addition, the acquisition of personal freedom for the criminal, in so far as it is related to loosening constraints, is then a part of the breakdown of society. Although the criminal gains equality, the concern for the good of the community is lacking. The criminal, with his new equality, is more likely to engage in antisocial behavior against the community.

The end result is that both sovereign and civic freedoms in the criminal justice system are diminished by the addition of the concepts of personal freedom and equality. It is easy then to imagine equality acting on a vertical hierarchy to weaken it, while trying to increase personal freedom. In such a case, that weakening would be a part of the harm done to the criminal justice system.

It is becoming more and more clear that the parts of our society that depend on vertical hierarchy and inequality are becoming more and more dysfunctional. Authors Fukuyama, Lowi, and Howard all refer to this problem in their books but fail to make the connection with personal freedom and equality. The connection is that vertical hierarchies depend on inequality, not equality, to function. Equality harms vertical hierarchies. Our society is rampant with inequalities that equality cannot eliminate without harming our country. This kind of creative destruction can only occur when we are unaware of the problem.

Education

In June 2006, a report on the state of American schools *(ED.gov)*, the National Center for Educational Statistics (NCES) Commissioner was quoted as saying, "U.S. students do relatively well in reading literacy . . . but they (high school students) trail many of our competitors (in other countries) in math and science literacy." In another report titled "How Does the United States Stack Up?" (March, 2008), the Alliance for Excellent Education states that "American education has stagnated . . . high school graduation ranks near the bottom . . . performance varies from mediocre to poor." In another report from The New Commission of the Skills of the American Workforce, the American educational system has "slipped to twelfth in higher education and sixteenth in high school graduation rates."

There were many other reports and articles on the Internet that portray our educational system as seriously in need of, at least, reexamination. Perhaps, the most damning statements come from the book *The Closing of the American Mind* (1987) by Allan Bloom. In that book, our educational system is described as being devoted to "liberating ourselves from . . . our taboos . . . that . . . are social constraints."

He explains this notion as a change from the original idea that truth is self-evident. The result, as Bloom depicts it, is a floundering educational system devoted to "openness." In this narrative, the idea of a troubled educational system is pursued in detail. The detail, in turn, provides an indication of a relationship between equal freedom for all and a weakening of our educational system.

It is true that the student–teacher relationship requires inequalities in order for learning to occur. When equality is applied in the classroom, it impacts the system in the same way as the criminal justice system. The treatment of students and teachers as equals slowly render the hierarchy dysfunctional, and learning occurs less frequently. It is well known that our educational system has been diminishing in quality for many decades. There have been many explanations for this phenomenon to blame the traditional educational system. For the most part, solutions are to throw more money at the problem or to implement new more progressive education. In this book, the real cause rests on an imbalance between inequality and equality with an emphasis on personal freedom.

One essential part of inequality between teacher and student is a teacher's ability to control and direct his students. In order to do this, the teacher, at times, must use fear and intimidation. Sometimes, this control function is veiled mild coercion with a smile and sometimes, it is blatant, direct anger. More generally, when fear and intimidation as an enforcer is deemed illegal or unfair, all inequalities and vertical hierarchies are weakened. Fear and intimidation have benefits as well as harm when they serve for the benefit of the community or family.

Take traditional education for instance; its core is a beneficial, respectful, and unequal teacher–student relationship. The teacher also uses unequal competitive testing to identify our best and worst students. Both mentoring and testing are based on traditional differences, which are inequalities that are part of a vertical hierarchy. Students earning high test scores are usually mentored by knowledgeable teachers and, therefore, earn high self-esteem, status, and prestige. Of course, this system is highly unequal. This traditional base is necessary for the efficient functioning of our educational system.

The concept of recognition, status, and elitism has been present throughout history as part of the authoritarian structure. Parts of what make the system work involve a subtle kind of reluctant respect for authority by some students. That respect is sometimes based on covert knowledge of the consequences of not respecting and obeying authority as well as the unspoken rules of vertical hierarchy. It also is based on the knowledge that the student can eventually become equal to the teacher through hard work and effort.

Any consequences, among other things, involve fear of retribution and veiled intimidation. That has been given for humanity since the beginning of time. When the consequences of challenging the authority of a teacher are based upon proportional disciplinary measures, the student will always weigh the cost of abandoning respect for authority.

The movement to apply equality and personal freedom to the educational system tears at the roots of the system by insisting that fear and intimidation are not necessary. Equality, literally, insists that punishment of any kind that utilizes fear and intimidation is unfair and cruel. As a result, a system without punishment and fear is weakened in its ability to do its job in spite of having achieved equality. You may have already guessed that fear and intimidation involve both benefits and harm.

One cannot solve the problem of fear and intimidation by eliminating the entire process, for the benefits are also eliminated. I do not believe that our current society can continue to exist without some formal acknowledgment that the inequalities of status and elites must be present in some form. It is also clear to me that fear and intimidation as a form of community good are an inequality that is quite necessary for the efficient functioning of our society. It is quite necessary to control and guide students in a classroom setting by using at least mild coercive methods at times. It is also important for the entire educational system to reinforce the unequalness of every individual teacher as he/she tries to help people learn.

Today, overall test scores have been falling for years, when compared with the scores of other developing countries around the world. At the same time, mentoring and testing are coming under fire because of their traditional beginnings. Recently, one high school banned homework, where homework is a bastion of the traditional work ethic. Although only one school has considered banning homework, it is ominous that any school would consider such a thing. The idea is particularly onerous as it is reasoned that because there is no proof that homework helps students, it should be eliminated. Surely this is no reason at all.

Everything traditional appears to be under mindless fire just because it is traditional. Now, it seems, all things traditional are suddenly associated with our modern falling test scores. Many traditional teaching methods are considered unfair just because they are not based on equality. The alternatives are, at least in some cases, no testing at all and/or teacherless education and learning through computer.

Although the teacher–student relationship is not, in any sense, like the master–slave relationship, it is still considered authoritarian because of the vertical hierarchy and its inequalities. Although the teacher has higher status and, to some degree, is the master, the student is not like the slave because his/her goal is to learn from the teacher and become equal to him/her. In other words, the student is not socially dead like the slave described in Dr. Patterson's books. Our modern student is a participant in a learning process and can strive for equality.

In the testing situation, society has a tool for determining inequalities between students. This tool offers students feedback about how much they are learning in their quest for equality with their teacher. Testing and report cards as important learning tools are losing ground these days because it identifies differences between students. This emphasis on differences or inequalities makes it easy prey for equality zealots.

In a sense, the modern alternatives all involve equality. When pressures are introduced to equalize the teacher–student relationship, blurring occurs and the differences between them are more difficult to perceive. The result is confusion, bad judgment, and unethical behavior. What should be happening in school is a cooperative synthesis of both methods that are based on good reason grounded in reality. Inequalities and equalities need to be assessed in realistic terms regarding whether they are necessary to the functioning of the system.

Equality in the teacher–student relationship is a goal in which the student, by hard work and mentoring, overcomes his/her unequal state. The more equal the teacher–student relationship becomes, the more likely conflict and anarchy will appear in the classroom. Each of us needs to accept the possibility that there are a lot of unequal things in the real world, which are beneficial in and of themselves. These unequal things usually require discipline. If one really wants to create equality in the classroom, all options should provide incentives to the student to earn his equality to his teacher.

The experience of having a responsible teacher or mentor that takes a personal interest in you as a student can be one of the most rewarding experiences in one's life. We also need to seriously question much of the babble through the media that condemns inequality based on a lack of equality. We need real reasons to resolve our problems. Equality alone is not a reason for excluding anything.

Public opinion is often given as a logical reason for doing things. It is often considered reasonable to do things, if other respected people do it. Remember, it was public opinion just a few centuries ago that stated that the world was flat. It was also public opinion before 1960 that African Americans should be segregated. Today, public opinion seems to be advocating eliminating our boring traditional educational system for a progressive completely modern system that makes students free and equal. Many people are shocked when such a system does not produce the desired results.

When public opinion becomes more powerful than the law, a radical blurring may occur. Our endless worship of mediocrity, through the belief in equality and public opinion, appears to be eroding our educational system. If you do not believe it, look over some of the books listed in the bibliography. The American educational system has been the cornerstone of liberty that is absolutely necessary for an effective and creative democracy. The intensifying attacks on traditional methods seem to bespeak a lack of respect for, as well as a mindless opposition to, traditional teaching and its testing as a method of measuring student success.

As the system becomes more equal and chaotic, intense stress on teachers may be encouraging some teachers to engage in behavior unheard of in the past. Teachers in increasing numbers are now actually molesting young students. This includes an increasing number of female teachers. The students themselves are demonstrating more behavioral problems. Students committing what seems like random murders in our schools are getting more commonplace. This new trend may reflect red flags as the bad behavior of our students and teachers increases. These trends appear to be slowly and subtly reducing the power of teachers and the schools, as it gets harder to tell the good guys from the bad guys, the predators from the victims, and the masters from the slaves.

As a therapist, I have personally come across an inordinate number of slow students who claim they were passed in spite of failing grades. This was so, apparently, because teachers apparently did not want these students to suffer reduced self-esteem. These kinds of decisions continue to occur even though it is a well-known fact in psychology that self-esteem cannot be given; it must be earned. These are some of the current problems with the educational system that are the result of the thoughtless application of equality and personal freedom over the traditional system. One should not have to be reminded that a slow student does not gain self-esteem from being passed without learning anything.

And so it goes, inequalities in the educational system are being covertly attacked by legal equality gurus that have no idea they are weakening the system. The benefit of the community is being decimated by the implementation of an old idea that only good can come from additional freedom and its cohort equality. Nowhere is the harm of progress, disguised as equality and freedom, considered. It does appear that the research that indicates a quarter of a century of deteriorating education is a valid concern.

Government

It is more difficult for me to describe American government because its popular image is one of free political networks serving the people. However, there is an abundant body of information served up primarily by the media that indicates political hypocrisy and chronic corruption. There are also several perceptive and well thought of scholars that have written on the subject.

I first became interested in government by reading a book from the past by Dr. Theodore Lowi. It is a difficult, but exciting book to read. A little background information is necessary regarding Lowi. In the late 1960s and throughout the 1970s, he wrote several popular books on political science; one was written in collaboration with Robert Kennedy. In 1976–77, he was listed by the American Political Science Association as "the political scientist who made the most significant contribution during the 1970s."

The main argument of his book titled *The End of Liberalism* (1969) is that liberal government grew to its immense size without recognizing its own problems in the 1970s. Liberalism, at that time, knew no political party as both republicans and democrats helped government expand and grow. The government was forced to grow in order to keep up with the enormous technological innovations of the time and the cultural developments associated with the civil rights movement. Part of that growth involved the formulation of policies that allowed a stronger alliance between government and special interest groups to form. That change to interest group liberalism was so drastic and so covert that he called it the Second Republic of the United States.

To Lowi, the new republic deviated so radically from our previous government and the constitution that he said "during the decade of the 1960s the United States had a crisis of public authority and died." He went on to say in chapter 10 of his book that "it (is) . . . relatively easy to show why . . . the Second Republic is . . . a bad republic and why it will ultimately undermine itself." The book itself is a turgid, complicated, creative venture that, even today, is a reading odyssey. In fact, much of what he says is even truer today than in his time. What follows is a kind of narrative regarding that book, with many of my own ideas added. Other authors are also mentioned.

Lowi goes to great ends to depict government by special interests as a government that uses increasingly bad judgment. The end result is that our politically bad judgment has caused us to move from a direct decision-making body to an indirect decision-making body. That indirect method by delegation embodies an increasing number of decisions in government that involve even more poor judgment.

The change, according to his book, is so abrupt that our politicians no longer abide by the original constitution. Do not mistake his conclusions as right or left wing fanaticism, since he was writing in a time when progressives and liberals were both democratic and republican. His conclusions were extrapolated from oceans of government data that he analyzed and he was backed by mainstream pundits and liberal scholars.

It is my conclusion that Lowi's narratives about bipartisan special interest group politics has now developed into a political liturgy for both parties. Not only that, the liturgy is now fully institutionalized and is now being implemented. It has been accomplished without a whimper or a giggle. What changes with each election is the kind of interest groups with which politicians relate. Further, the theory presented now proposes that the political changes that occurred in the 1960s were the result of our government's inability to govern the rapid expansion of the general culture.

I would add that there are similarities between the American Republic and the old Roman Republic. A big difference, however, is that the Roman Republic imploded and then melded into an authoritarian state. On the other hand, America has devolved since 1960s into something totally alien to our original republic. We have become that, which we were originally against. We are topsy-turvy.

As I see it, we have divested ourselves of the First Republic's goals and constitution in order to become a swarm of political special interest junkies. On an abstract level, we are being affected by our belief in equal freedom for all, and at the same time, practically, we are loosening constraints and applying equality in every aspect of our society. In fact, our politicians today are not even aware of a problem as they scamper on, interacting increasingly with special interests.

In the meantime, they twist and spin their words, all the while assuring us that they are on our side. Simply put, our politicians are much less on your side and more on the side of the ever-changing landscape of special interests in the Second Republic of the United States. They are, more than anything else, confused.

In the case of larger or smaller government, the politicians in charge are easily corrupted, believe in loosened constraints in most areas, are increasingly lenient, exhibit poor judgment, and are thoroughly grounded in the fairness of equality. They usually deny their beliefs in public unless these beliefs are part of their false extreme ideology.

Yet, Lowi has said that the question of more or less government is remote, for "we already have more (government) and (our) democracy will tolerate nothing less." He goes on to say "the complexity of modern life forces congress into vagueness and generality in (the) drafting (of) its statutes."

The ideology of both political parties believes that a lack of constraints is of tremendous benefit to prosperity. Most of us have held those beliefs, because historically, they have been mostly true. Yet there are limits, even to freedom. It appears to me that we are rapidly approaching these limits. Since corruption appears most prevalent in politics, it is fair to speculate that political parties are likely to be lacking more in constraints than other organized groups. That is why they are more corrupt. Alas, there does not seem to be much in the way of hard data with which to compare corruption and harm in government with other institutions. However, there is formal logic, and the corruption that appears to us as news.

In order to portray our current republic in a weakened state due to equality and loosened constraints, some discussion is necessary. There is a multitude of rather subtle coercive political forces, which interact with outside special interest groups as well as formal government agencies. The bones on which these forces adhere is called patronage. It originated in ancient times in both authoritarian and democratic governments that knew nothing of modern equality and personal freedom.

However, patronage of the old type is very much alive in modern American politics. The practice of patronage is largely assumed, and few even question it. Still, patronage in America is quite different from the Roman version. In America, patronage is all gussied up and disguised so that it looks democratic. American patronage is defined, in this book, as the power to grant political favors.

In a book by Cullen Murphy called *Are We Rome?* (2007), patronage is described in detail regarding how it was used in Rome. Then, the author goes on to compare patronage in Imperial Rome with patronage in modern America. He did that in spite of the obvious fact that Imperial Rome was authoritarian and America is democratic. It is my thought that the earlier Roman Republic would have been a much more reasonable comparison.

Murphy explains that originally under the Roman Republic, the Latin word *"suffragium"* meant "ballot." The idea is that earlier, in the Roman Republic, the general free voting populous held a certain amount of power by ballot. That, to some extent, meant that there was a "sense of reciprocal duty" present. In other words, a kind of equal respect by the sovereign senate justified favors and gifts for some of the general free population. That same general population then held a mutual respect for the senate and a feeling that they were freer, more prosperous, and safe than before.

Murphy went on to say that this early idea of partial equality changed when Rome replaced the senate with an emperor. It changed again when the empire fell. The word *"suffragium"* then came to mean "the pressure that could be exerted on ones behalf by a powerful man." Apparently, Imperial Rome patronage, "bread and circuses," and low taxes as the means for keeping the masses motivated and participants in the empire. That was all part of sovereign freedom.

At the same time, Roman law became a stronger tool for free Roman citizens to benefit from civic freedom, as long as they lived within the law. Of course, both of these freedoms involved horrific inequalities that, at least in the beginning, seemed fair some of the time. Still, Roman patronage seemed to work best in the beginning when there was a kind of partial equality and a motivating spirit. It also seemed to be at its worst when the empire ended and no equality existed.

But things eventually went "horribly wrong" after several hundred years of Imperial Rome. As Murphy states in his book, "by empires end, all public transactions (patronage) require(d) the payment of money . . . (which) gradually remove(d) . . . any sense of public spirit . . . and replace(d) it with an attitude of what's in it for me." Murphy goes on to relate that . . .

> "it goes to the heart of the question that is starting to be asked in America, where some form of degenerative . . . condition has left government responsive to particular special interests but deaf to the popular will."

It seems as though Murphy perceives public spirit in America wavering as greedy concern for money and materialism co-opts American politicians much as it did in Imperial Rome. But Cullen goes on to seemingly place blame on businessmen and private sectors for corrupting our politicians. He did that in spite of the fact that many special interests are not about businessmen seeking profit. Considerable government special interest money also is being allocated to government agencies and nonprofit corporations. He also admits that "private contractors may be able to operate more efficiently than government agencies do."

To him, the Roman patronage problem resides in the distortion of communications from the sovereign to his general population. In Imperial Rome, there were few special interests, as we know it. Rome, at that time, was an Agrarian society that considered business and businessmen of low

60 | Floyd Sours

status. In addition, there were no nonprofit agencies like Acorn or union special interests. It is hard to imagine that businessmen or special interests were to blame in Imperial Rome since they either did not exist or they were considered lowly.

For Murphy, the breakdown in community "spirit" results from privatizing government functions. Strangely enough, that is exactly the same argument that our government is using now. Our politicians blame corrupt capitalists for our predicament. The result is distrust of private business and corrupt behavior by some. This is all done without any real evidence that corruption in business is any worse than it is for politicians or the general public.

At the same time, the organized group that seems most corrupt is our politicians, unions, and nonprofit organizations who are our new special interest groups. Apparently, the sovereign's fair and just messages were distorted in Rome as they cascaded down the vertical hierarchy. To Cullen, they are distorted in America because these underling businesses have lost their sense of public spirit due to privatization and profit motive. A sense of fairness has been lost.

It seems to me that Murphy, in his zeal to blame private business for the demise of our vertical hierarchy, is overlooking the real problem. I think he, at least, realizes that the vertical hierarchy of government patronage is being corrupted. I do not, however, believe that blaming privatization and business is the answer.

In Murphy's world, our politicians would behave with more virtue and business savvy if only the evil businessmen would not tempt them. He has no clear idea that people who function in a vacuum must surely become corrupt, if only to avoid being bored. Put those same people in a tempest, and stress will make them even more corrupt. Our politicians live in a self-imposed political pressure cooker as they give themselves luxurious jet planes and expensive vacations and parties, and grow rich when we are all losing our jobs. That shows clearly that they are not in tune with the average American.

They have affairs, covet interns for oral sex, visit prostitutes, swap wives, get drunk, entice interns for homosexual favors, buy political favors, do not pay their taxes, take bribes, abuse illegal drugs, and tell us lies about what they are doing. In spite of this, Murphy offers us a penetrating observation of the American problem but offers questionable solutions to the problem.

It is true that some businesses are partly corrupt, for they, like politicians, are largely self-regulating. It is also true that politicians and governmental agencies are not only corrupt, but they are inefficient and exhibit bad judgment. If you do not believe it, read Dr. Lowi's *The End of Liberalism* (1979) or Howard's book *The Death of Common Sense* (1994). What Cullen does not see is that the corruption by government is a natural result of a democratic government corrupting itself. It is similar in some ways to the Roman Empire.

Our American democratic government did not collapse like the Roman Republic. The Roman Republic ceased to exist, but our government has been slowly degrading itself since somewhere in the middle of the twentieth century. Our government itself has become extremely wordy and fuzzy in its language while delegating actual authority downward to the very persons delivering or creating the product or service in question. They no longer describe things in a way that makes things clear. Our politicians are no longer direct and specific about what legislation will do, what it will not do, and who will do it. Yet their legislation has gotten wordier, while saying less.

The extremely poor judgment in government agencies, wordiness, and detailed legalese is also depicted in Howard's book. Many examples of government misjudgment and waste are clearly portrayed. Both Lowi and Howard point out corruption in government agencies that has been ongoing for a long time. Increased detail without clear planning and goals "has increased in the Federal Register from 15,000 pages . . . in the Kennedy administration to over 70,000 pages in . . . (the elder) Bush's administration." The point is that the more detail and specificity that are provided for a government of law, the less we have a government of men making fair clear rules from good judgment.

The clear message is that our politicians themselves seem to represent the most corrupt group of all, but the corruption has become so common that we all pretty much accept it. We are desensitized. Lowi surmises that real excessive corruption and bad judgment in government have been around since perhaps the 1960s. My thought is that our country has become so sophisticated technologically, particularly in communications, that our politicians and our government agencies have become quite dysfunctional. They are unable to maintain control. They are so mired in detail that they no longer are able to control the country.

Our country has expanded and grown to such an extent that our government cannot keep pace. In an effort to keep up, our politicians have attempted to become more effective by delegating money and projects to private special interests. Businesses have generally done a better job than our politicians and government agencies. It is my thought that politicians did not privatize things consciously, but group decisions about specific problems brought about possible solutions slowly by delegating them out. This is easier to understand when it is realized that our politicians are more like used car salesmen than they are like businessmen or philosophers.

It is pretty clear to me that organized entities that have less constraints will become corrupt. However, most businesses, including small businesses, remain responsible and still use good judgment. Politicians, stock market,

62 | Floyd Sours

and business are the three areas that are affected more than most by loosened constraints. In the case of politics, there has been little, other than our constitution, to stop them from acting unrestrained except for group process and public opinion. According to Lowi, since 1960, they have not even been constrained by the constitution. It is the nature of mankind that we have structure and reasonable constraint, particularly in times where harm and chaos prevail.

Oftentimes, the patronage system is the conduit for corruption. After all, the patronage system itself is a bastion of unequal sovereign freedom by a bunch of political aristocrats. On the other hand, the equal give and take called reciprocity is supposed to be contained within the patronage system. It is a contradiction in terms: on the one hand, we have equality in reciprocity and on the other, we have inequality in patronage. Taken together, they could be regarded as a weak sovereign.

No wonder our country's government lags far behind the rest of our society. The patronage system itself is a leftover part of authoritarianism. Our elitist politicians work hard to create the illusion that they are just like us—equal. The hypocrisy is that politicians are notorious for saying one thing while doing another. As the politicians and special interests interact through patronage, corruption increases as participation gets more unequal. By that, I mean the elites, our politicians, and special interests become more and more unequal to responsible citizens. They work deals and become rich, while the average American is impoverished slowly.

The patronage in Roman-style authoritarian government was dependent on reciprocity originally. It was one of the few means to enhance the senate's sovereign freedom for its semi-free citizens. When Rome became corrupt, community spirit flagged and Rome was no more. American democracy, while having patronage, is a far different thing.

In western civilization, there are many ways for politicians to promote community spirit through reciprocity. Patronage is but one of them. While politicians have indulged in patronage since America began, the media has increasingly portrayed it as corrupt. It has always been regarded as an elitist political process that requires inequality and a covert elitist attitude on the part of our politicians. The American patronage system, as it presently works, is a veiled vestige of Imperial Rome encumbered by the broad general cultural forces spreading personal freedom and equality throughout our land. It is a contradiction in terms.

Those broad cultural forces of equal freedom for all do not realize that they are weakening the political patronage system. In the same sense, the politicians themselves do not see their system crumbling. They do not even know that the institutionalized patronage system is unequal. Because it is presently corrupt, it is not participating with the general population in

Burnt Offerings | 63

any honest and equal way. It is for that reason that the spirit of freedom is diminishing, while elitist politicians romp and get rich.

As they work in a pressure cooker of their own making, they must constantly praise the common man in an effort to appease him while keeping their elitist views under cover. Their public talk is, as Shakespeare once wrote, "words and music signifying nothing." The solution to this patronage problem is very clear. The congress and the president, without manipulation or intimidation, must listen carefully to the American people and initiate clear and direct legislation, which incorporates the average man's ideas into it. That is what is meant by ground-up decision-making and true reciprocity.

As an afterthought, it is important to note that politicians can enact legislation that the public wants or needs. They do not have to do what the public wants all the time because some of it is either impractical or harmful. In fact, they would be accepting of just a few of these things. In order to stay out of trouble with the public, politicians must not become defensive and cut off communication. They should be able to explain why something cannot be enacted or implemented in a convincing fashion. Two recent presidents seem to have had a talent of maintaining their popularity in the face of crisis. They are Bill Clinton and Ronald Reagan.

When the community good through reciprocity is lost to greed, the entire idea of equal relationships is lost to a covert unequal hierarchy where greed and riches are the new goal. I should add that real reciprocity is between real well-meaning and informed politicians and the general populace; not special interests. I do not think that reciprocity of that kind is dead; it is just sleeping. What there is of reciprocity is the most well-kept secret in the world. It seems as though community spirit, exemplified by participation, is under a covert attack. Politicians today are highly manipulative as they use "smoke and mirrors" to deceive the public.

The more divided our political groups become, the more conflict is contained. Conflict resolution does not occur easily because many people in congress are involved. Our politicians often are stuck and frustrated as they obsess over details. Soon these politicians become rigid and stubborn as they descend into confusion. In order to avoid the anxiety of getting nowhere, the participants indulge in the new goal of profit-taking and greed. At least, it feels good.

These kinds of things exist because neither politicians nor special interests have much meaningful structure with which to operate. Those guidelines that do exist were mostly created by politicians themselves. Further, our governmental patronage system has evolved into a covert vertical hierarchy based on inequalities. That includes the patronage system, but the public is not yet aware that patronage has any harm at all associated with it. So with few or no external constraints, politics has corrupted itself. The truth is that, like education and criminal justice, government also has its unequal hierarchy. In this case, it is much more hidden from public scrutiny.

Mental Health

There are some other areas where inequality exists that do not fit into the previous groups. Mental health is one such area. At one time, the inequalities between therapist–counselor and patient–client were rife with conflict. This conflict peaked in 1970 with the publication of *The Manufacture of Madness* by Dr. Thomas Szasz. In that book, Dr. Szasz shocked the mental health community by likening inpatient psychiatric care to the inquisition.

The patients were likened to witches, and the doctors were portrayed as church inquisitors that tortured and often killed their patients. In that book, the point was made that today there is much inequality present just as there was in the inquisition. As a result, in the doctor–patient relationship, meaningful communication had difficulty occurring. There was only one-way communication where the doctor always won.

Today, forty years later, therapists and counselors work much harder to be peers and friends to their patients. While that more equal approach is certainly an improvement, beyond a certain point, it blurs the distinction between normal and abnormal behaviors. As time goes on, it is harder to identify diagnostic categories from normal behavior. That is because the therapist often becomes too close and bonds with his patient.

As a result, the therapist/counselor is often unable to continue to be objective about his patients since the boundaries between them have been diminished. Generally, in the mental health field, there is considerable disagreement among professionals about the correct diagnosis for the same patient. This disagreement is well documented in research and tends to indirectly support the idea that boundaries are being diminished.

This discussion brings home the problem of equality versus inequality. Dr. Szasz narrated an argument that more equality would promote more effective treatment in mental health. To a certain extent, that probably was an improvement, but the blurring effect of relating more closely and equally to a patient also has its harm. It is my belief that treatment in the mental health field has been improved by more equality in the therapist–counselor relationship. Still, the data, what there is of it, does not bode well for highly effective treatment.

When the unequal relationship between therapist and patient has equality imposed upon it, therapists and patients similarly lose some of the sense that there are personal boundaries between them. While people lose some of the sense of identity, they gain a sense of involvement as they become better friends. That involvement is more intense emotionally because there are fewer official boundaries. The loss of boundaries eventually may result in the inability to differentiate one person from the other. In such a case, sameness pervades the relationship as both persons feel less lonely.

The loss of personal boundaries creates extremely emotional allegiances, which involve either (or both) love or hate. Persons caught in this kind of equality web often eventually engage in violence against others or themselves. And so it goes, beyond a certain point, equality can create harm in interpersonal relationship as well as benefits. As we equalize the unequal relationship between therapist and patient, it becomes more and more difficult for professionals to determine a diagnosis and distinguish between normal and abnormal behaviors.

The perception of equality diminishes the separate condition that enables us to distinguish boundaries between things. It is boundaries between things that establish certainty, trust, and confidence we have in our relationships. Those boundaries for centuries have contributed to the stability of close interpersonal relationships.

That means that an involvement by any two people in a relationship can become too intense or close. That closeness, in turn, may make them unable to see the other objectively because the perceived boundary between them has become blurred. The participants cannot tell where they end and where the other begins. For therapy, such a condition can be disastrous.

When we become closer to people, they seem more equal to us. At the same time, our superficial unequal perceptions diminish. We are left with strong emotional attachments that involve either love or hate—not both. Professionals constantly have to manage the detached unequal perception against the deep emotional bonding that accompanies equal relationships when they engage in treatment.

In a sense, the relationship is phony and superficial because the professional must continually detach as he reexamines his impersonal diagnostic codes in the light of the patient's behavior. The therapist's own feelings may also interfere at this point. He does his diagnostic thinking and still professes a peer relationship. The relationship may be more emotion-laden and primary than his objective diagnostic skills and the patient's behavior. His developing, more profound understanding of his patient is literally beyond words after a certain point.

In actual fact, the professional is not able to become as close and be as equal as a mother would be to her daughter. The mother obliterates the inequality between her child and herself. She engages in unconditional care, without any pretense of overriding rules and reason. In this case, the relationship can verge on delusional, as all boundaries disappear between them and equality is the king. The closer we come to equality in relationships, the more blurred objectively determined boundaries become. While there are relationships based on equality, when unequal relationships exist and equality is imposed, the result can be blurring.

Dr. Szasz also spent some time depicting the awful conditions of the lunatic asylum. It was clear that asylums and psychiatric hospitals were definitely unequal. He likened the old-time asylums and modern psychiatric hospitals to the jails and prisons in the dark ages where witches and heretics were tortured and killed. The point was that these prisons and hospitals housed unfair constraints on heretics, witches, and the modern mental health patient. His book in the 1970s was unbelievably successful, since all of us were aware of the atrocities from the past that had occurred under tyrants wielding horribly unequal law.

Strangely enough, about the same time Dr. Szasz published his book, the community mental health movement appeared. The goal of that movement was to move the mental health patients who were trapped in the psychiatric hospitals to the community where better treatment could be available. In other words, the horrible inequalities and constraints of the inpatient setting were to be eliminated and patients then could receive voluntary unconstrained outpatient treatment in their community. The problem at the time was that research was mixed about whether freeing the mental patient would produce better treatment. Undaunted by the lack of research, the powers that be decided equal freedom should be adopted anyway.

Psychologists and psychiatrists in the state hospitals were kept very busy discharging mentally ill individuals into the community. While this was all happening, there were numerous facts that did not make the news. One such incident was when fifteen to twenty discharged patients died in a nursing home fire. This incident was in the news but it was not mentioned that the occupants were discharged mental patients. Another incident occurred when the state of Illinois decided not to increase the money to outpatient mental health centers to accommodate the increase in populace in the community. They did that even though they had originally promised to support the movement. The result was, surely, an increase over time in the number of homeless people in the community.

There was no need to suppress information about increases in crime, drug abuse, and mental illness because no one thought it was connected to the mental health movement. For sure, equality was on the move as psychiatric facilities across the country reduced their number of patients radically.

The point is that equality was served as patients were discharged from highly structured inpatient units to a voluntary outpatient service that was less constrained. That is true even though the state legislature did not increase the money available to the communities in which these patients were discharged. Apparently, they liked the idea of keeping the money.

Burnt Offerings | 67

Since I worked at the time in both inpatient and outpatient facilities, it was clear to me that the professionals working in the state hospital setting were more unequally authoritarian than those working in the community. Those hospitals also were highly structured and many patients had been committed involuntarily. In this case, the patients were literally "freed" from the clutches of unfair constraints by discharging them into a more open community that had fewer constraints and more equality. The belief at the time was that the community would be a healthier environment because there was more equality and freedom.

The message is clear: the old system was on the ropes as the mentally ill were unshackled and made more equal. The question is whether treatment was actually improved and whether, at a certain point, the application of equality together with loosened constraints weakened the system and/or the community. The jury is still out on that because no good data that I know is available. There is some circumstantial evidence, however.

In Stanton Peele's *The Diseasing of America*, success rates in mental health treatment that average around 75 percent are discussed. He also related that the research also depicted treatment benefits galore. But he states that most of those studies were conducted without control groups that did not go through treatment. When the 75 percent of success is compared to the 60 percent success rate for persons not using mental health services, it appears that a marginal 15 percent average success rate is the real benefit of treatment.

I should add that surveys and rating scales abound in the researches that explain increased employment, lowered divorce rates, and reduced sickness that are benefits to diagnosis and treatment, so there are other benefits than treatment success to consider. It is my thought that success in treatment is not as high, on average, as most people think. Further, treatment success is likely higher for depression and anxiety, but lower for drug addiction, sociopaths, and psychotics. In some cases from the latter groups, research success rates were negative, suggesting that patients got worse with treatment.

In regard to whether the mental health treatment system is being harmed by the encumberment of equality and loosened constraints, there is little data. The number of untreated potential users of mental health treatment in America (National Institute of Mental Health, 2007) is about ninety-five million annually. This figure combined with the ninety million annually who do receive treatment suggests that a large segment of our population (185 million) is diagnosable and in need of treatment. From that data, it is suggested that well over one third (at least 37 percent) of our population could use treatment. It does appear that there are a lot of people who are mentally ill in America.

68 | Floyd Sours

Unlike the statistical ratio regarding the benefits and harm of driving cars as described earlier, the benefits of treatment in mental health seem low, and harm is unknown. A large number of people who are diagnosable and potential recipients of treatment suggest that a large problem exists. Available statistics are only able to suggest fairly ineffective treatment and a large part of our population that is mentally ill. If that is true, then it is possible to imagine that the mental health hierarchy is being affected by the equal freedom for all movement. Perhaps, the effect of all this equality that impacts chauvinism in the mental health system is also associated with poorer treatment results.

Summary

If you have followed this diatribe to this point, you know that the last few sections have depicted governmental control moving from direct control to indirect control by manipulation. The examples given suggest a general weakening of the control function in education, in criminal justice, and particularly in politics and government. Weakening could also be true in the mental health field, although statistical data is sparse and often nonexistent.

Although government and politicians are more complicated, their problem with bad judgment may have begun in the 1960s. Politicians have become increasingly corrupt and government agencies have become more indecisive. The result is that those decisions they have made have often reflected silly misjudgment. One example in the news some years ago was a government agency that bought screws for several hundreds of dollars each.

It is my thought that what really has happened is a loss of control, leaving no one to steer the ship. Numerous writers in the recent past have made reference to an "out-of-control" system, but none has attributed it to our ideas of personal freedom, equality, and constraints. Stanton Peele (1995) thinks the medical community and the media are to blame, Lowi (1979) attributes it to corrupt government, and Allan Bloom (1987) associates it with a faltering educational system. There are other authors as well, with a plethora of statistical data and theories. Lowi and Howard both illustrate convincingly that politicians and their government agencies may have become out of control first, with it worsening with the passing of time.

7

Good and Evil

Good and evil, reward and punishment, are the only motives to a
rational creature.

—John Locke

No practical narrative on equality and freedom can proceed without a
discussion of the unintended consequences of applying them to our culture.
One such harmful consequence is the rapid extinction of the ideas of good and
evil in our civilization. This book has already implied that the inequalities
involved with the idea of good and evil is intimately involved in our current
cultural problems.

The idea of good versus bad in the western world originated with
pre-Christian philosophers like Plato and slightly later with the Christian
religion. The early Christian influence, in particular, developed the idea
further as Christian ideas osmosed into the laws and rules of the civilizations
that were home to Christians. The Christians often referred to good and bad
as good and evil.

As western civilization has matured, the positive emphasis on goodness
and the corresponding negative emphasis on badness have become a basic
ingredient of western society. These ways allow us to make judgments on
individual and group behavior as to whether a given behavior is good for
society or not. The dichotomies of good versus evil were transformed over
a long period of time into use and abuse, normal versus abnormal, rewards
versus punishment, and guilt versus innocence. Each of these dichotomies,
at their core, distinguishes between good and bad behaviors in society.

By emphasizing what is good and what is bad behavior, we have learned to
generally improve society by rewarding good behavior and/or punishing bad

69

behavior. In an efficiently functioning society, behavior has consequences, and not all behaviors are equal. In fact, an efficiently functioning society must distinguish between good and bad. Of course, that distinction is highly unequal.

The concept of good and bad began to change rapidly in western civilization in the middle of the twentieth century. Indeed the concept has been rapidly diminishing, as equal freedom for all has been applied as part of an increasingly secular American society. The point here is that there are a lot of unintended consequences developing that are harmful to our society. These symptoms, at a practical level, involve everyday decision making throughout western civilization. However, the basis of each of these paradoxical terms is derived from the distinction between good and bad. All of them rely on inequalities to work effectively.

Justice Lost

Let us use a specific saying that Lowi uses in his book. At the end, he mentions the "bull in the china shop." He relates that:

> There is a bull in a china shop. Suppose the shop is filled with objects so ugly that the bull could give us great pleasure by smashing the place to bits. Yet though we may be pleased, we cannot judge the action of the bull.

While it is stated in Lowi's book that no judgment can be made, it is not clear why that is true. It seems to me that Lowi means that no judgment can be made about a bull or a china shop until good and bad is superimposed onto the descriptive metaphor. As he says, "they (the bull in the china shop) bear no relationship to any esthetic principle."

Lowi states, "without the rule (good or bad), the whole idea of justice is absurd." When no distinction is made about what is good and what is bad, the saying has little meaning. As a result, no judgment can be made in regard to the bull or the china shop because there is no concept of good and bad built into it. In fact, without good and bad, no court of law in which guilt or innocence is decided can make an honest judgment if only descriptions are offered.

Without the idea of good and bad, no one can utilize a rule in order to make good decisions. The concept of good and bad is a moral imperative that allows judgments to be made. The saying only describes the problem that needs judgment; what is good and bad is imposed on the description and then a judgment can be made. Traditionally, our legal system has utilized the distinction between good and bad to frame laws that identify good and bad behaviors in our society.

The law then determines appropriate rewards for beneficial behavior or punishment for harmful behavior. The law makes sure that there are consequences for our behavior, and our civilization continues. The goodness or badness of any event can be superimposed over any problem for which laws or rules are used to determine a just solution for all. Laws, like the saying itself, have little meaning without distinguishing between what is good and what is bad for the community. This notion is the core of what is called civic freedom as well as common law.

If the "bull in the china shop" metaphor was present in a totally secular society without the distinction of good versus bad, no judgment could be made about the problem it represents. If we assign the bull's behavior the designation of bad because of its potential for causing damage to the china shop, then a judgment can be made. Furthermore, the designation of bad for the bull's behavior automatically designates the china shop as good. A law then can be created that deals directly with the problem and protects all china shops from the damage caused by bad bull behavior.

When this happens and a law is created, the focus of attention by the law is on the safety of china shops. As a result, any bull in a china shop exhibiting bad behavior will be duly punished under the law. The designation of guilt or innocence embodies the idea of good and bad. Such an embodiment assures a just attempt at problem resolution for the sake of the good community. A law then can be created for any problem situation so that the law protects the good of the community. What is always assumed to be present is the inequality of good versus bad, which is incorporated into the law. Unfortunately, in modern America, we seem to have forgotten the good of the community.

The whole idea of the law supposedly has been to focus on protecting the good of society, while punishing bad behavior. As I understand Lowi, he thought something like that was true until sometime in the middle of the twentieth century. Prior to that time, congress had a committee for almost all laws and their agencies acted as overseers that directly administered the law. But Lowi thinks things changed radically in the sixties of the twentieth century when the law became less specific and more indirect. Congress also loosened constraints by providing much less oversight.

Howard's book, *The Death of Common Sense* (1994), also narrated case after case of really bad judgment in government agencies that were trying to make decisions based solely on law without a moral imperative like good versus bad. It is my thought that as equality was implemented across the land in mindless fashion, a shift of attention occurred. This shift was to the bad bull's behavior, instead of the safety of the china shop. The rights of the bull were called into question with that change in focus.

72 | Floyd Sours

Two things happened as a result: 1) the bull's bad behavior was diluted by attributing good or neutral underlying intentions to it and 2) the focus on equality insisted that all living things that exhibited similar bad behavior be treated equally or uniformly. This new focus is now on the process of focusing on bad behavior almost exclusively rather than on the good of the community. It represents a concern about whether fairness is present for those exhibiting bad behavior.

In real life, the first example could be likened to the compassioned plea of the Menendez brothers, who murdered their parents, saying that they were abused by their parents at an early age. The bad behavior of murdering their parents is compromised by the perception that they were treated badly as children, thereby inferring that they were somehow partially justified in their behavior. The problem with such an argument is that *intentions* are difficult to measure or prove. In the case of the Menendez brothers, the parents are deceased and cannot speak for themselves regarding whether such abuse occurred. The good of the community, in this case, is compromised by a focus on the brother's behavior and intentions.

In the second case, the focus on *equality* for bad behavior between living things simply makes it impossible to pass judgment at all on the bull's goodness or badness. A real life example of this can be seen in our insistence on equality for criminals, illegal aliens, and responsible citizens. By insisting that they all must be equal, we avoid the argument that responsible citizens have a right to special treatment as defined by civic freedom. Under civic freedom, those citizens who followed the law are given special unequal freedom.

Today, the pressure for equality evens out inequality without even a discussion. It diminishes the inequalities of civic freedom under the law. Rather than deal with that inequality, it is ignored in the pursuit of equality. The result is a secret assault on law and civic freedom that professes the goodness of equality as its goal.

There is no critique of this movement as criminals and illegals gain undeserved freedoms described as equality as an end in itself. Soon all three will be so equal that one cannot tell the difference between the good citizen, the bad criminal, and the illegal alien. This shift from the good of the community to the process of determining the fairness of all bad behavior has its goal to assure fairness to all while ignoring that responsible citizens have traditionally had advantages over others. This new trend ignores the fact that civic freedom has almost always helped make communities and nations more stable.

Howard's book has a myriad of examples of a turgid focus on process that makes judgment difficult. It is a matter of focus, for the human mind can only attend to one thing at a time. The shift is to the process that one engages in before judgment, rather than on deciding guilt or innocence. That shift to formal process also happens in law when the focus is on making all school districts equal in funding or equal in percentage of different ethnic groups. It ignores the possibility that the systems being equalized are also being weakened. This reminds us that there is now a serious unarticulated cultural problem developing in America.

This problem is created by the erosion of unequal imperatives from the ordinary legal descriptions that describe current law. Without the assignment of unequal good and bad behavior in law, one is left with only descriptions. Without moral and ethical imperatives, the descriptions themselves cannot determine right or wrong. Our federal government and its politicians are particularly guilty of flooding federal agencies with legislation filled with descriptions without imperatives. Howard's book (1994) gives example after example of that kind of bad judgment in government agencies.

Howard's book is filled with egregious examples of agencies that are unable to make wise and good judgments. It is my contention that these agencies are operating on descriptive statutes. No wonder they have delegated responsibility and authority to private special interest groups who can make judgments more effectively. This whole section suggests that the federal government and its politicians have, for many years now, been dysfunctional and unable to perform their duties. The current corruption is the result of their dysfunction.

Blurring

Authoritarianism in crisis breeds rigid constraints, zealous despots, and rigid personalities. Democracies under stress become more adaptable, accommodating, and open. Too much adaptability and accommodation creates a quite different outcome than rigid structures. Blurring, as an outcome, can be just as destructive as rigidity. Blurring is defined in this narrative as the process of making things dim or vague.

Blurring indicates that there is too much general emphasis on sameness or similarities. Instead of differentiating between things and establishing boundaries that provide conceptual clarity, similarities between things are pursued. Beyond a certain point, boundaries become vague and less clear. In our modern age of excessive information, blurring becomes a cultural problem and also becomes as problematic as excessive rigidity.

Everyday in the media, we see good guys being shown as bad, and bad guys being good. The result is a growing inability to distinguish good from bad. Thus, our citizens in general are losing the basic sense of inequality as a result of blurring. This kind of blurring, in my opinion, can be likened to a

74 | Floyd Sours

cultural psychosis if it gets chronic enough. Differences between things that have allowed us to make fair judgments in the past are now becoming lost to blurring (see Table 2).

In Table 2, the relationships between blurring, democracy, and similarities are presented as phenomena that tend to occur together. Rigidity, authoritarianism, and differences are also presented as tendencies likely to increase and decrease together. In this book, blurring is the new idea because, to my knowledge, no one has taken time to speculate on whether human perception varies according to the culture.

Blurring and Rigidity by Kind of Government

Kind of Government	Perceptual Extreme	Mode of Thought
Democratic	Blurring	Similarities
Authoritarian	Rigidity	Differences

Table 2

Unlike the past, it is now more difficult to tell the difference between good and bad. In blurring, boundaries breakdown as constraints are lifted. It is more difficult to differentiate between things. Serious suppressed cultural problems have a tendency to resurface when barriers and boundaries are breeched and eliminated as modern blurring occurs.

Racism

We appear to be losing the past, but we are not gaining the future. That is true because we are focusing on something other than solutions and justice. Part of this shift of attention involves justice as applied to the concept of racism. When one plays the race card, as in the old O. J. Simpson murder trial years ago, judgments regarding innocence and guilt are affected. Racial prejudice, as an accusation, shifted the focus in that trial from the defendant's bad behavior. By doing that, the defense attorney was able to shift attention to the police and law enforcement. The implied suggestion was that the police may in fact be bad instead of being good. They may be racists.

This shifting of attention not only suggested racism, it also undermined and weakened the entire criminal justice system. Even if racism were present, the evidence of Simpson's guilt was still overwhelming. By focusing on law enforcement instead of the bad behavior of Simpson, the good of the community is diminished. A weakened criminal justice system and a weakened community are a symptom of the cultural illness that is slowly turning things upside down.

It is my contention that the criminal justice system has been affected generally by this kind of shift, and racism is becoming more of a witch hunt where authorities are increasingly wrong. The O. J. Simpson trial was only the tip of the iceberg. America needs to take stock of itself and acknowledge that most things have benefits and harm. Even using the race card has its harm. All of us need to be more aware of attempts to digress from issues of guilt and innocence by shifting attention to the process leading up to final judgment. Issues regarding racism and the underlying goodness of bad behavior should be carefully scrutinized before they destroy the entire process that leads to justice.

The Evolution of Inequalities

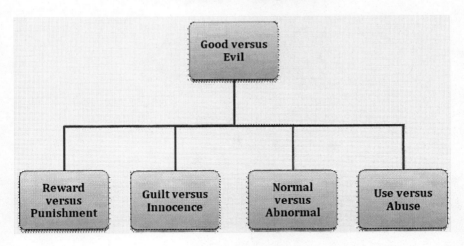

Diagram 1

And so, we conclude this section by highlighting the offshoots of good and evil (see Diagram 1). It is clear that guilt and innocence, rewards and punishment, normal and abnormal, use and abuse, and many other inequalities are the descendants of the original good and evil. These inequalities and the older, more basic idea of good versus evil are all under attack in our society by the concept of equal freedom for all.

Some popular nonfiction books, over the last century, have clearly identified the problems but have not related them to equal freedom for all. Perhaps it is time to come out of the cave into the light in order to consider the consequences of what we are doing to ourselves. As Pogo, the comic strip character once said, "I is seen the enemy and it are us."

8

Bad Judgment

Men of ill judgment oft ignore the good that lies in their hands,
till they have lost it.

—Sophocles

Lately, politicians and government agencies have been portrayed in a rather negative light because of perceived corruption and bad judgment. Much of the reasoning behind such a depiction is attributed to investigative journalism and the data presented in a few well-known books from the past. What is new in this section is the premise that political bad judgment is the result of a government that has been unable to keep pace with our rapidly expanding general technological and scientific culture.

A part of this bad judgment is the slow demise of the historical duality of good versus bad. About a half century ago, statutory law in our increasingly secular society expanded—particularly in government. Since the duality of good and bad is unequal, it is being diminished in our society by the forces of equal freedom for all. The result: it is increasingly difficult to distinguish between good and bad in our society. It is all partly the result of our government's inability to keep pace with the rest of our culture. As Lowi relates, "life is on the decline . . . because government structure has become incapable of dealing with modern social problems." It is now important to speculate about how we have become politically dysfunctional.

Law and Government

At the present time in government, political elites and their archaic agencies are constantly on the defensive as they deny their own aristocratic attitudes, veiled ideologies, and personal corruption. There is an inherent hypocrisy in our politicians as their words clearly do not match their deeds. Even the way they bargain and interact smacks of deceit as they utilize their unequal patronage system secretly to profit and secure status and recognition from special interest groups.

The truth is that the patronage system that now exists lost the spirit of reciprocity long ago. Yet it is supposed to characterize democratic patronage. What is left speaks more to greed and inequality as coercive manipulations than anything else. Moreover, there is little transparency and meaningful communication, as this thorny brew is more and more suppressed.

In order to grasp the larger view of a deteriorating government and impotent politicians, it is necessary to digress a bit. For the first hundred years of our country, common law governed relations. Howard (1994) in his book then relates that "statutory law began to replace common law." He goes on to say that "at the turn of the (twentieth) century, when the progressive movement began . . . statutes began to dominate."

Statutory law involved a trend toward increasing legal detail that was so rigid that the rules allowed for no exceptions. As he said, "the words of law expand(ed) like flood waters." The goal was to create increasingly detailed statutes in an attempt to give us all the certainty we lacked in a dysfunctional government. No common sense human judgments were to be included because the law covered it all. Our modern law makers were suspicious and untrusting of human judgment. As statutory law increased, reliance on human judgment decreased.

Thus, human judgment that incorporates the inequalities of good versus evil cannot assist law in determining the common good. In the purely secular world of statutory law, all human judgment is bypassed, as laws mechanically try to cover all possibilities with the written word. Human judgment and human error have no place in such a uniform equal world. Without human judgment, the boundaries that define unequal, legal interpretations become blurred as injustice rears its ugly head.

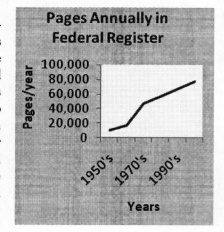

Graph 4

As was mentioned earlier, the number of pages in the federal register of our government, as compiled by the Office of the Federal Register, is depicted in Graph 4. From its early annual 2,620 pages in 1936, it slowly increased and then really accelerated in the 1960s until 2008 when congress produced eighty thousand and seven hundred pages (see Graph 4). The number of pages increased phenomenally from fifteen thousand pages in the early 1960s to over eighty thousand and seven hundred pages in 2008. As Howard related, "Federal statutes and formal rules now total about 100,000,000 words (and that was in 1994)."

With mountains of detailed statutes to lead the way, there is no distinction that can be made between good and evil. The people who used to make those distinctions have now been eliminated by professional bureaucrats whose bible is the agency policies, procedures, and statutes. All of this has occurred without the mandate of elections, polls, or law. The proverbial bull in the china shop has been stripped of all meaning without any communication to the American public.

Small Groups

This narrative now will proceed to describe the small groups in politics. Such a narrative will provide a close look at governmental bad and good judgment in groups. In a book called *American Politics*, author George McKenna (1976) described the American political scene through the eyes of a partisan liberal in the 1970s. In the first part of that book, he astutely depicts a process that he describes as the socialization of conflict. His idea of free and open communication as it relates to decision making is covered rather well in that book. It was apparently the result of the trials and tribulations of the Watergate Affair in the early 1970s, and it has a decided liberal tilt to it. Still, the author's description of the relationship between freedom of speech and decision making is invaluable, yet incomplete.

McKenna begins by portraying democracy as conflict management. As he says, "democracy always leaves open the possibility that at any time, the circle (of controversy) may greatly expand, that the number of participants (in the conflict) may be greatly enlarged." He makes it clear that conflicts in an authoritarian government are contained within a small ruling clique and, in general, conflict is suppressed. On the other hand, a democratic government is mentored by its citizens and "facilitates the spread of contagion." His example was of a conflict starting with a narrow circle of elites, which expands to others. If the problem is not resolved, it finally may even become a concern for the whole of society. His example is quoted as follows:

80 | Floyd Sours

"The critic of a government agency might first try to work within the agency itself . . . getting nowhere, the critic might then bring up the matter behind the closed doors of a congressional committee . . . finding the committee mainly interested in sheltering the agency from criticism, the critic may persuade a member of congress to bring it up on the floor of the house or senate . . . if the criticism still fell on deaf ears, he or she might turn to the media . . . (it would then) become a public controversy . . . (where) governing officials (are held) to the sword of public accountability."

Liberty, for McKenna, is "the means by which (a) self-governing people keeps itself informed." He used the word "liberty" often in the same way I have used the word "freedom" in this book. He goes on to say . . ."the best way to find truth in the political arena is through the free trade in ideas." He goes on to describe the kinds of coercion that disrupt freedom of speech.

I would add that he seems to think that all forms of coercion are harmful to freedom of speech, since coercion alters or structures the free flow of speech. He even goes so far as to call these forms of coercion restraints on idea trading. It seems to me that he is trying to say that if only these restraints could be eliminated, then full personal freedom of speech would be the result. In fact, he does state that "liberty is sometimes defined as absence of restraint."

Equally important is the continued emphasis on unrestrained freedom of speech that diminishes the effectiveness of our leaders and their laws in government. In other words, it is an emphasis that diminishes our more traditional sovereign and civic freedoms. The idea of providing a forum for all who wish to communicate appears to have developed into a forum for ideas that are extreme, brief, interesting, and simple. Any moderate or centrist ideas are not even considered, presumably because they are less interesting.

McKenna's earlier example of conflict resolution in a democratic society was based on the use of continuing additional participants in a conflict, the longer it remains unresolved. The example was the Watergate debacle in the early 1970s. The inference was that this process would work all the time in all situations. The conflict, as it went on, began to involve the general populace and public opinion. It was supposed to be an example of freedom of speech and personal freedom, as it was contrasted with authoritarian governance and censorship. It was also an attempt to explain democratic mentoring where the general populace gets involved in the problem-solving process.

It presumed to show how freedom of speech brought down a corrupt sovereign. The entire narrative was based on the premise that President Nixon and his cohorts thought they were above the law by engaging in criminal behavior against their political opponents. Another way of saying it is that

Burnt Offerings   81

they were engaging in aristocratic manipulations that were unequal; thereby, breaking the unwritten law of equality.

In this case, it was obvious that Nixon was a villain—not a hero. In either case, he was using the inequality of special privilege as sovereign freedom. He was free to do as he wanted since he was the president. President Nixon was operating behind the veil of secrecy, using the unwritten custom of traditional politics to implement plans behind closed doors. The constraints that represented sovereign freedom were portrayed as being political custom and executive privilege. It was clear that those constraints needed to be removed.

Just as the private group process of Nixon and his cohorts was supposed to be traditional political custom as constraints, the public arena of free speech was the antidote. In actual fact, his example, which only consisted of involvement of the larger group of people, only worked for an abuse of the system. Conversely, beneficial use of political custom was not even addressed.

Authority and responsible persons using the system properly for beneficial ends could be stifled and rendered impotent if that same process is utilized under normal conditions. It looks like public oversight only works when abuse is involved with the primary group. The point is that *freedom of speech*, as a political deterrent, *only works to remove abuses of the system.*

In the case of responsible use, the expansion of freedom of speech into the public arena can be harmful. The public idea today seems to be that open, transparent, free speech is the solution to political problems. In other words, if a private group process is occurring, then open public free speech about it can only enhance the process. The idea that private group process can be harmed by free speech is missing.

Further, making problems public, as a means to solve problems, has not worked like McKenna described it for other problems. For the democratic process and freedom of speech, open communication in politics may lead to communication involving people that may make decision making impossible. It does surely result in the containment of conflict and the resulting indecision. Let us now look clearly at group problem solving as it relates to free speech.

In our democratic society, a small group of elites usually begins by collecting information regarding a problem. Usually, a group process unfolds where each member is assigned a part in the information-gathering process. In some groups, members are allowed to delegate information gathering to designated people or agencies. Members and their designees are all encouraged to participate in the process. These participants are usually rewarded by recognition, status, or money. Each member brings his/her information and ideas to the group, and conflict between them is accepted.

After a certain amount of time, alternatives are presented with each being rated in order of importance. Then, a final choice is made, based on majority rule. The group leader or facilitator may then represent the final result giving credit wherever he sees fit. As you can see, a democratic group allows considerable equality between members, while the other, more authoritarian groups, involve inequality. Yet the democratic group still has some inequalities because some are necessary for the efficient functioning of the group.

Although outside public sharing of information beyond the group is not ordinarily accepted, the possibility of outside influence is ever present in a democracy. In fact, the pressure of outside influences is so great at times that secrecy has become a problem. In fact, in our modern democracy, it has recently become a problem to keep a political secret at all. Members of these kinds of groups are keenly aware that if things go bad and information about the group go public, all kinds of outside pressure for more information may create an extreme public position, which is in total opposition to the group's original position and/or purpose.

As the number of additional outside participants gets bigger, the opposition may get more intense. The stronger the opposition, the more pressure there is to reveal more information about the internal workings of the group as well as their plans for conflict resolution. The original goal of resolving the problem is now unworkable and the goal unattainable. In addition, the distinction between public and private has become blurred, as it becomes increasingly difficult to tell the difference.

The example given in McKenna's book was that of the 1972 Watergate break-in. This was not a conventional group of people trying to resolve a problem. This was instead, a group of elites meeting to abuse the system as well as the group process. Initially, there was the perception that the president's group was responsible. The new shift in perception was that they were abusing their own system and essentially were small time crooks. In politics, at least, it seems that the use of public information to uncover government abuses can work.

However, it would not work if government officials were honestly trying to resolve a serious problem in the right way, while persons outside that group were suspicious of the group's workings. That is because that group would be responsibly using the political system, not abusing it. In fact, having its internal workings and purpose going public could decimate a responsible group with an important purpose.

There is, it seems to me, an increasing irrational tendency to regard any political problem-solving group as suspect. That is particularly true when public trust of politicians is low, as it is now in America. Even our politicians have no trust as they investigate individuals and groups of the opposing party

Burnt Offerings   83

regularly. There is also a tendency to think that the public has the right to any and all information. What follows is an example of responsible political group problem solving that should *not* be subjected to public scrutiny.

In the book *Essence of Decision*, Graham T. Allison (1971) mentions the well-known internal group dynamic of the Kennedy administration's decision to blockade Russian ships during the Cuban Missile Crisis. Because the book is technical and detailed, I will not spend much time on it. In general, it portrayed the Kennedy administration following the rules for democratic group problem solving, as related earlier. While, in this case, the conflict was resolved successfully in a very high-risk situation, my point is that freedom of press in this case would have completely destroyed the group's goal of successful conflict resolution. By focusing on a group's possible abuse, one shifts attention from the original goal of the group.

For any group, a focus on process can obliterate or at least weaken any group's goals. When that happens, we would all better hope we are right about the group's abuses because that group is now unable to function effectively. The real question is how we, as free citizens in a democracy, decide whether use or abuse is occurring in a political group when the federal government makes decisions.

Freedom of speech should not be taken lightly for it has its benefits, but we should not presume that there are only benefits. It appears that Americans have a natural bias as they conceptualize all private groups as though they need public oversight and transparency. This bias seems justified when it is explained as a right under freedom of speech but it also plays havoc with private specialized group process. In the long run, it can produce a blurring of the distinction between group issues as it produces bad judgment.

It does appear that the pressure of equal freedom for all provided an effective solution to the Watergate problem where a secretive authoritarian president was misusing his sovereign power. In our zeal to apply equality everywhere, we all quietly assume that all group processes would be enhanced or at least corrected by transparent open communication.

Since considerable harm could occur to government decision making, it behooves us all to grant the inequality of political custom where responsible plans and solutions are being developed. These traditional inequalities are a part of sovereign and civic freedoms and deserve to continue as long as they are engaged responsibly in the country's best interest. Instead of adhering to the sure perception that public oversight is beneficial to all group process, we need to first hone our ability to determine accurately where harm is being done.

Instead of generalizing oversight to all groups, we need to focus on ways of identifying kinds of abusive groups. We need to know initially if these groups are significantly different from each other. If they are, they are not likely to be easily compared. Oftentimes, differences are a reason to designate each entity as a kind that is unequal in composition.

In the case of political group process, that designation of kind is all important if good judgment is to prevail. By designating kinds, it is no longer possible to speculate that all groups need oversight. Some kinds of groups may contain unequal qualities that may make them untrustworthy without reason. If we get good at defining kinds of groups and defining them, then the potential harm of oversight will be diminished. As an aside, we should not forget that the democratic group process is an innovation that has benefits and harm.

Even in political groups, the inequalities that involve sovereign and civic freedoms are very much alive, but little is spoken about it. Sometimes, the thin air of few constraints produces secret irresponsible plans and actions. Politicians are well known for their bad judgment and corruptness, but many still function responsibly on our behalf. You, as citizens, need to know the difference.

9

Losing the Magic

> A republic, if you can keep it.
> —Benjamin Franklin,
> when asked what kind of government had been created.

I think we can all agree that bosses, teachers, employers, and other authority figures are necessary in our world. We probably all would also agree that some laws and hierarchies are necessary. It is just that we do not recognize those elements as belonging to the authoritarian realm and, as such, require inequalities. It is equally hard for us to envision a world without hierarchies, law, and authority figures. When we do imagine such a world, it includes only freedom and equality for all.

Nowhere do we see freedom and equality as harmful. Disorganization, meaninglessness, boring uniformity, and alienation are not thought to be connected to equal freedom for all. Based upon the ideas discussed earlier, it is my thought that the ideal of an open democratic society without structure is a recipe for eventual disaster.

Throughout our history Americans have advanced freedom as a loosening of constraints and prosperity has followed. That is particularly true of capitalism as free enterprise. When we try to eliminate too many of the constraints that hold our culture together, all hell breaks loose. All the while, we are losing the feeling of being secure and protected because it is the solid structure of these constraints that allow us to feel protected.

If we want to be maximally secure and protected, we need competent authority and responsible law in tandem with equal freedom for all. We also need to begin accepting a kind of creative thinking that can provide new beneficial structure that melds with existing structure peacefully.

86 | Floyd Sours

Today, we seem to be destroying existing traditional structure without any thought about the consequences. The idea of vertical structure and unequal relationships is absolutely necessary for the continuing effective functioning of government. It also is necessary for our own mental health.

The mindless application of equality and the harm it produces needs serious reexamination. Equality is not fairness and it does not produce self-esteem. It definitely is not a part of reason or logic itself. Even science requires discipline. The loosening of the shackles on the dominated is not an idea that is easily generalized to the rest of the world.

We cannot go around loosening constraints everywhere expecting prosperity to follow. The harm, which accompanies it, is America's dirty little secret. Still, the benefits are many, as people dance to the tune of prosperity. The solution is an improbable marriage: a compromise between the modern forces of equal freedom for all and the traditional forces of unequal freedom through benevolent authority and responsible law.

America has come a long way in just a few years. In the last several centuries, we have conquered the western frontiers of North America, generally led exploration into space, added several states to our union, fought and won most of our wars, and experienced the highest standard of living known to man. Generally, this has been attributed to the spirit of equal freedom for all.

While all this has been happening, our politicians and government have degenerated into a corrupted conflicting bunch of elitists who make up their own rules, engage in grossly unethical behavior without remorse, and covertly make allegiances with special interests in order to become rich. They clearly are unable to govern fairly on our behalf. Furthermore, their reliance on extreme ideologies that do not represent the people flies in the face of common sense. They are like the true believer that Eric Hoffer described years ago as, "men whose personal failings lead . . . (them) . . . to join a cause even at peril to . . . (their) . . . life-or yours."

It should be noted that politicians are often elected to their positions on "hot" social issues that include equal freedom for all. Because they are elected for a particular stance on an issue, they ordinarily do not let reason modify their position later. Often, in my opinion, they make up their mind before they know anything about the subject and, in fact, fall far short of ever considering the unintended consequences of their actions. Our politicians are not known for their introspective qualities.

Of course, the essence of being elected intensifies the importance of group opinion for them. Any elected politician must keep his ear to the ground about what those who elected him want. He also must compromise himself constantly with his fellow elected politicians and their ideology. Most of them also create allegiances with special interest groups. Considering the constant social pressure to conform to a myriad of pressures, it is no wonder so many of them are corrupted and utilize bad judgment. Rather than uphold what they consider right, it is so much easier to coerce, intimidate, lie, and manipulate. In a way, they are slaves who have no master.

Because there are few rules, except group pressure, many of them increase their personal wealth and power by supporting dubious causes through special interest groups. It is also true that special interest groups are constantly changing and include many equal rights groups, educators, unions, nonprofits, as well as businesses. In essence, any group that is big and rich enough to pay lobbyists to market their issues to congress and the president is a special interest group.

Social Freedom

That brings me to my main point. The social issues that politicians bring to the political forum are, for the most part, wrong. Often these issues are the pet project of some special interest that stands to profit considerably from its enactment. It is conflict of interest at its worst. Politicians are usually on one side or the other of any social public issue. In terms of logic, only the extremes are presented. Only one or the other is right. What is supposed to happen in a democracy is a compromise between combatant politicians. Our politician's stance on any issue is only meant to frame the conflict; it is not meant to be a solution in and of itself.

For many years now, America has been locked in political conflict with little or no resolution on major issues. In many of our current political conflicts, the current solution that is offered is an extreme position. At the present time, a huge political majority can ram through partisan solutions based on a thoroughly questionable ideology. At the same time, because of extremely rigid political partisanship, no compromises can occur. This ideology will not motivate private business, nor will taxing them further future expansion. It is all politically designed to ingratiate a flawed ideology that is extreme. It all smacks of bad judgment by a group of political true believers.

Each of the following social issues represents opposing extremes in conflict. Neither extreme alone can resolve the conflict, only willing compromise will work. The extremes only frame the conflict; they do not resolve anything. The answer is in the middle where most American citizens reside. These issues are highly associated with personal freedom and the lifting of constraints and equality on one hand and constraining authority and law on the other.

Each of them is opposing extremes that define the problem and each is in conflict. Each extreme is aware that their issue has obvious benefits. The problem resides with the lack of awareness of harm embedded in each side's myriad benefits. Some of the issues of personal social freedom and equality are as follows:

- The legalizing of illegal drugs
- Equal rights for criminals, citizens, and illegal aliens
- Laws, rules, and policies designed to produce equality in our school system
- Laws allowing, eliminating, or modifying abortions
- Laws about freedom regarding sex and child bearing for females
- Laws and policies making it more or less difficult for employers to hire and fire employees
- Laws designed to equalize inequalities between administrators/managers and employees
- Laws designed to alter the consequences to the environment caused by human innovation
- Laws about surveillance and control of the population
- Laws designed to equalize marriage and family
- Laws restricting or allowing free trade in the time of crisis
- Laws expanding or constricting mental illness and drug abuse treatment for any group of people for whom success in treatment is not documented by good research.

This list is not comprehensive and does not describe the extremes but it does give some sense of the areas in which work needs to occur. Our politicians often throw back specific stances for many of these issues to the general public in order to get elected. They often present one extreme, not a compromise, as a sign of progress. The opposition often takes the other extreme. The reality is, according to this book's premise, that neither extreme is an acceptable solution.

It is clear to me that equal freedom for all embodies both equality and the loosening of constraints. Equality, in particular, is a veiled ideology that is saturating our society mindlessly. As such, it is producing obvious harm. That liturgy is in great need of critique to bring the idea out in the open and to forge rational boundaries for its use. It is this author's belief that going too far with extreme positions will jeopardize our democratic future. In a sense, it publicizes our inability to find reasonable solutions. We are, I think, on the verge of losing the magic, which has served us so well in the past.

It is important to reiterate that the benefits of freedom and equality are many. However, the unintended consequences are particularly destructive because it is a phantom illness. Many people acknowledge high crime, rampant drug abuse and mental illness, easy divorce, and schools that do not teach. These same people fail to see that the deterioration of our culture is directly related to the amount and kinds of freedom and equality that we have as a democracy. At the same time, freedom and equality are the direct opposites of the responsible constraints that authority and law uphold. That, to me, is the harm of freedom and the unfairness of equality.

Politics as Usual

As we come to the end of this section, Dr. Patterson's words from the past remind us that "the uniquely western chord of freedom . . . has always existed . . . (as) . . . personal, civic, and sovereign freedom . . . (in an) . . . often fragile unity." In America, today, personal freedom and equality rings discordant against the background of sovereign and civic freedoms. In modern American politics, the lack of harmony is most obvious as the heroic *equal freedom for all* prince *attempts to slay* the two-headed *sovereign and civic freedoms* dragon. The result, to date, has been the evisceration of organized authority and law.

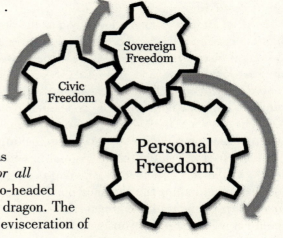

There does seem to be a recent political movement that is including more sovereign freedom in government. That movement is touted by the current politicians that have taken over politics in a big way. However, since the premise of this book is that sovereign freedom must coordinate with the other two freedoms, only a sovereign that does not degrade the other two freedoms is acceptable. In order for harmony to occur, several things are necessary.

- ◦ First, any political authority must effect honest communication with the general populace, conjoint with any legal solutions. These solutions must include some of the masses' needs and wants.
- ◦ Second, special privileges must be supported for law-abiding citizens in order to facilitate civic freedom.

90 | Floyd Sours

° Third, no extreme ideology should be enacted without compromise with its opposition.

At the time of this writing, none of these unifying issues are in process of being enacted.

So the meanderings of this book have offered a clear picture of a world in need of unity. Personal freedom and its cohort, equality, are careening across America benefiting and harming everything in its way. The old civic freedom may yet be destined to the dust bin of history as equality reduces the privileges of citizenship to meaninglessness. Although sovereign freedom seems on the upswing as progressives enlarge their political sway, their inability to openly communicate with the general populace and their ideological rigidity make unity more difficult.

All in all, things do not look good as the possibility of war looms large on the international landscape. As always, war is the ultimate last ditch unifier when all else fails. The sad reality is that if we cannot unify ourselves, then international chaos and war are the primitive alternative. As usual, the chordal harmony of freedom escapes us. Yet it is only in America that such unity or harmony could be fully developed.

The answer to the question about how to make our democracy a better and happier place for its citizens lies not in making everything equal. Instead, it also involves reinstating basic inequalities like good and evil and all of its modern offshoots. We need to be able to identify the good and the bad as the first step in pursuing the good and combating the bad. In order to do that, we need clear boundaries defining terms—not blurring. We also need to become aware of the unintended consequences of any proposed progress. For it is all too common for most of us to view progress as only having benefits.

Modern psychology and the Christian religion have juxtaposed the idea that good and evil are each present in the same person. At the same time, it is also proposed that external individuals or groups may be entirely good or evil. Psychology, in particular, has explained evil as the result of the individual's upbringing or immediate circumstances. These kinds of ideas have presented problems for the religious notion that evil can be inherent in a single person or group. The traditional idea is that a person involved in an evil deed always intends to do evil. In psychology, people engage in evil with a variety of intentions. The idea of intentionality causing bad behavior philosophically is a more difficult idea since intentions are not easily observed or measured.

In this book, an evil deed speaks for itself as bad, regardless of any individual's intentions or circumstances. If an evil deed is performed, the person or group owning it must suffer the consequences regardless. The enforcement of such an idea is dependent on fair authority and just law-wielding rewards and punishments. Generally speaking, any human behavior that is considered evil is also bad for the community, the nation, or mankind. Laws and fair authority must punish bad behavior swiftly and fairly regardless of personal intention or circumstance.

The end result of fair and firm legal enforcement would be a society that is moving closer to the three kinds of freedom resonating together in harmony. Equality and inequalities should function side by side in a community that accepts both as potentially good. So this chapter has been a critique of America as it succumbs to chaos. Its ideas about freedom desperately need reassessing in the light of different kinds, but perhaps, more importantly, the idea of inequality should also see the light of day.

Perhaps, we are now witnessing a historical change where America is losing its edge. It seems to be losing that traditional optimism that characterized Americans through two world wars. Yet perhaps, this is only a pause for adjustment as we go onward and upward to a new age. Only time will tell.

10

Synopsis

In the End is my Beginning.
—Mary, Queen of Scots

This adventure called Burnt Offerings has produced a number of new ideas. They all were spawned by dividing one idea of freedom into three different kinds. It all then boiled down to the idea of equality versus inequality; for, two of the kinds of freedom require unequal cultural conditions and one requires equality. The book is filled with vivid new visions and everyday examples. These ideas and examples are a new way of looking at things. By building on these new perspectives, several new ways to look at cultural problems that seem almost unsolvable are presented. Each of these problems is summarized as follows:

Cultural Anxiety

Perhaps, the most controversial is the idea that *authoritarian governance provides a feeling of being protected and secure.* That feeling occurs because sovereign freedom allows but one unified belief and censors and punishes all others. When a pluralistic democracy such as ours is superimposed over a more natural authoritarian core, *the feeling of protection and security is diminished as the more equal personal freedom becomes a reality.* In our democracy, countervailing beliefs and conflicts of all kinds are allowed that are anxiety provoking and alienating for the individual. While allowing these conflicts public access, the premise is that we can solve these problems together. It is also theorized that *some people, by experiencing these unpleasant*

92

feelings, become more mature through adversity. This kind of maturity cannot be obtained under an authoritarian regime.

When political ideologies conflict, politicians and citizens alike can polarize and become very rigid. We all are locked into a static, anxious mess where everyone becomes more alienated. The more one ideology tries to eliminate the other, the more anxious and rebellious the average person becomes. Obviously, the answer is to solve the problems, but half the answer lies with each ideology. Because of their rigidity, the polarized forces are stubbornly unwilling to compromise.

All the while, *citizens and some politicians are trying to participate more* in local governments, charities, political parties, state governments, and religion. They do this in order to relieve their existential anxiety by creating organized human structures that can solve problems. In other words, they *recreate the structure that has been taken away at the federal level.* That new structure, however, is decentralized with many groups contributing. The result can be a more creative, well-organized, productive, and less anxious society.

Dueling Opposites

Another concept proposed in this book is the idea that *there is logic to conflicting opposites that can evolve to problem resolution.* It is proposed that the increased participation created by anxiety is the result of loosened cultural constraints and the application of equality. That increased participation, then, not only provides structure, but can develop conflict between organized groups. When public awareness of the conflict peaks, the public takes sides. Often, these conflicts are political in nature because politicians are interested in these various social positions in order to be elected.

As was quoted earlier by Fukuyama regarding the philosopher Hegel, "the desire for recognition initially drives two primordial combatants (master and slave) to seek to make the

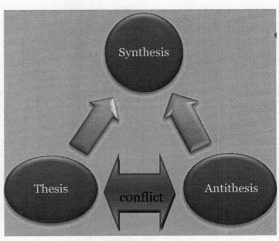

Diagram 2

other recognize their humanness by staking their lives in a mortal battle." In the modern world that battle involves, not only humans, but ideas as well. In fact, Hegel in his complicated way proposed that beliefs evolve in a particular way (see Diagram 2). First, a belief is articulated and a group is formed. He then proposed that when these beliefs become known, their flaws also become known. Others, as they begin to understand these flaws, form their own opposing group. The two groups then conflict in this mortal battle. The idea is that over time the groups evolve and the conflict resolves itself by compromise. According to the popular version, the original group is the "thesis" and the opposing group is the "antithesis." When the compromise unfolds and the solution is evident, the end result is called "Synthesis" (see Diagram 2).

The entire process, as it evolves, is rather difficult and ruthless, but history depicts many human conflicts that make this dialectic credible. The problem with such a theory is that the two combatants can regress to war or murder. When groups or individuals do not compromise, they often become rigid and defensive to the point of murder or war. This kind of regression is a characteristic of authoritarian government.

However, because much of America, including our politicians, is still basically authoritarian, this participation often results in fearful rigidity by conflicting groups. Positions by opposing groups then become so rigidly polarized that political problem resolution is nearly impossible. On the other hand, for the minority of people who have an ideal democratic mind-set, blurring becomes a problem as they no longer can easily identify good and bad, guilt and innocence, or normal and abnormal behaviors. Blurring, as a process, either diminishes to the point of clear perceptions and rational thought or it becomes worse to the point of chaos. Individuals living in chaos may then experience a radical regression to the point of authoritarian rigidity.

The rare individual who is neither blurred nor rigid sees reality clearly. He is Dr. David Riesman's autonomous man from *The Lonely Crowd* (1953) who is neither inner-directed nor other-directed. Autonomousness means an individual who is adaptable enough that he/she can take the best of each opposing side and propose a compromise solution. In American politics, such a solution is called bipartisan. The ideas of rigidity and blurring are extreme perceptions that necessarily distort reality and produce bad judgment.

In this book, the primitive battle to the end is described as a regression to the ancient master–slave relationship. If no compromise occurs and the conflict is contained too long, blurring or rigidity occurs. For authoritarian groups, rigidity results in stubborn, defensive opposition and later regression to a primitive battle to the end. In the case of democratic blurring, distinctions between things are no longer clear as bad judgment becomes more evident.

A kind of mass psychosis can occur if blurring continues with no problem resolution. If too much blurring occurs for too long, a radical regression will occur to a rigid authoritarian state. For either extreme, bad judgment occurs and any polarized opposites stand anxious, in need of a solution.

The idea present here is that *problems are solved in human culture by the evolution of conflicting groups.* If solutions do not occur, either group can regress to a primitive state where one group wants to destroy the other. In this state, the groups polarize, and then one group aggressively attempts to eliminate the other.

There is another rarer option where the two conflicting groups maintain reasonable communication and attempt to arrive at compromise solutions. Usually, the logic of opposites does not come to a full compromise solution until considerable conflict is engaged in by both primitive conflict and rational compromises obtained through on-going communication. As a last resort, the primitive battle eliminates the opposition and it is regarded as a short-term solution. Still, in the long run, other opposing groups may form to begin the conflict again.

There is one last truly global observation that can be extrapolated from this narrative. Instead of proceeding mindlessly forward for progress, America needs to determine what the secret to our success was, by evaluating our past. If that secret involves inequality, so be it. If it involves bolstering authority, our system of laws or individual discipline, then we would better acknowledge it and reward those who engage in it properly.

America must pause from our mindless race into the future armed with progress and cry of freedom. We must seek out the benefits of the past and give them their rightful place in our society. In doing so, we must compromise ourselves for the benefit of our brothers who believe differently. This would constitute a new direction than the one called progress that we now pursue.

Benefits and Harm

Other food for the mind's eye comes from frequent references to the consequences involved in cultural change throughout this book. When most cultural changes occur, often only benefits are envisioned as the result of those changes. In this book, the idea is advanced that *with any cultural change, both benefits and harm develop.* The lack of consideration for any harmful consequences is thought to be a cultural bias. Of course, the opposite bias also occurs, such as when environmental zealots envision only cultural harm from environmental changes.

It is even stated in this book that the ratio of benefits to harm can give us useful objective information about cultural change and how it is impacting

96 | Floyd Sours

the culture. The example in this book is a practical calculation regarding the impact of the automobile on our culture. The result of comparing the number of licensed automobile drivers to the number of drivers killed in the same year suggests a minimal amount of harm and a large number of benefits.

Apparently, the innovation of the automobile allows considerable freedom of mobility for individuals while having a low percentage of harm to drivers. Throughout the book, inferences and suggestions are made that either benefits or harm were not considered as consequences for numerous cultural innovations. In the end, the idea of a ratio of benefits to harm gives us a way of measuring the impact of a change on culture. It is also clear that any cultural change, even an idea that produces change, can be estimated or objectively measured. The ratio, as described, constitutes a new simple law of benefits and harm.

Power Corrupts

The idea that American government is corrupt and uses bad judgment is not a new idea. Several books have been written about it. Yet in this book, a new concept has been introduced as it theorizes that our present government, including both political parties, has lost their way. Our lost politicians are dysfunctional because the rest of our culture has radically expanded in the last half century. Our modern culture is likened to the ancient Roman Republic that probably imploded from such a rapid expansion. Although our culture has not imploded, our politicians have been corrupt for years. Additionally, the formal government agencies that our politicians oversee have been using really bad judgment for years. Both seem to be unable to make decisions much of the time. They appear to be too rigid and defensive—a sign of authoritarianism.

The premise is offered in this book that continual bickering and poor judgment in politics has gradually produced a corrupt and unreasonable politic. Since the satisfaction of solving a problem is not obtained, corruption and bad judgment is the result. It is also theorized that neither the ancient Roman Republic nor our current American democracy had or have any real constraints placed on them. Perhaps, the lack of constraints is the reason for that old saying "Power corrupts."

In our case, we did not implode because we have terrific scientific technology, strong local and state community organization, and creative business enterprises. However, since power eventually corrupts when reasonable constraints are not present, the *political corruption is the result of a lack of constraints.*

The answer for us is to elect some honest people who are not easily influenced. They then should organize some short clear legislation based on what the public wants, and then implement it responsibly. Each time that is done, our politicians will feel the satisfaction anyone feels for doing a good job. If that does not happen, then perhaps, the American public should be put in charge of politicians salaries and enact a law that makes receiving money or gifts from any special interests illegal. Clearly, our politicians would not willingly pass and enforce this kind of legislation. However, it may not be too hard to do if the general public consistently voiced their approval of such a thing while electing more honest, strong politicians.

The Good of the Community

Part of this book was spent describing how the law has experienced a perceptual shift from laws that protect the good of the community to laws that evaluate the kind and amount of bad behavior the defendant exhibited. The new perspective can involve various ploys such as intent or a concern for how the defendant was processed for his alleged crime. In any case, the concern is now on the process and not on the good in the community.

The point is that as this new focus gains momentum, the old focus on the community is weakened. It is proposed that not only is harm done slowly to the good community, bad judgment creeps into the system as judges no longer use moral imperatives. The good of the community is lost to imposing equality on the criminal and the responsible citizen. Although there are benefits to focusing in the courts on processing the defendant and on analyzing his bad behavior, there is harm done slowly to the community and criminal justice system. Such *a proposed relationship between weakened communities and a focus on process in law* is proposed in this book.

An Ending

It is not necessary at this point to say that the concept of equality, not only has a politically controversial definition, but it is also the central focus of this book. It is clear to me that all of the other new ideas presented in this book depend essentially on equality and constraints.

Equality as an idea is necessary in order to define the legal boundaries between each individual person. The partnership of legal equality with freedom then becomes the method of assuring evenness of distribution for freedom between people. At the same time, legal equality is also an obstacle to the attainment of full absolute freedom for all individuals. In this way, *equality acts on uneven and unequal relationships to reduce or eliminate them.* As this is accomplished, equality also works to constrain coercion and intimidation of one person or group over another at least temporarily. The problem is that only containment is achieved as contrasted to solving problems.

In America, today, we have an unlikely marriage between equality and freedom. The idea of freedom is unitary in that only personal freedom is considered and then only a lack of constraints is really popular. That unitary vision allows Americans to have a specific opinion about many things in our culture. The unitary vision, for the most part, leaves out any consideration of ideas involving law, rules, authority, and individual responsibility.

An example of how equal unitary personal freedom impacts on a specific cultural problem are the issue of freedom for illegal aliens and criminals. The argument is that they should have the same rights as legal citizens. The singular idea of freedom is to give those groups more freedom and equality. They should legally be as equal and free as legal citizens. In order to do so, we must be more lenient and lift harmful rules from them. We do this because freedom means that we loosen the constraints that were put there as punishment for engaging in illegal acts or for coming to our country by breaking the law.

If it is believed that there are different kinds of freedom, this problem takes on a whole new meaning. Civic freedom means being a responsible citizen living under the law. It is an unequal freedom that gives special privileges for abiding by the law. Criminals and illegals are excluded in an unequal way as punishment for breaking the law. This is an entirely different view of what in this day and age is a controversial problem. Seemingly, unsolvable problems now have the possibility of being solved by utilizing the idea of kinds of freedom interacting together.

In the case of civic freedom, the unequal status of citizenship makes it possible to consider special status for responsible citizens. That concept is the traditional understanding of citizenship. It strengthens our culture. The new unified popular version that most Americans now consider reasonable has never in all of history been considered an acceptable solution.

At the same time, the modern idea that responsible citizenship, which has traditionally been considered a community good, is viewed with suspicion. People are suspicious of it, in spite of the fact that it has been a part of our freedoms since the beginning. The current unitary concept has little potential for solving the problem of the good in the community. It also makes our criminal justice system more lenient by reducing the intensity of the punishment meted out for bad behavior. Our world is turned upside down by a single idea of personal freedom when all of history could not do it.

Unequalness combined with sovereign and civic freedom can illicit new and better ways of understanding a cultural problem. A clear example of this is our current political stalemate regarding whether we will treat terrorists as criminals under civil law or under military tribunals. Here, we have equality acting to equalize the terrorists with the American citizen. Once again, the obvious special privileges for our citizens are downgraded to equality. The reasoning is that all people, even terrorists who want to kill us, should have the same rights under the law. This belief is only right if you believe there is only one kind of freedom: personal freedom defined as a loosening of constraints. On the other hand, if you acknowledge sovereign and civic freedoms and their inequalities, the special privileges of citizenship can be seen as good for the community.

Envisioning our culture through the prism of three kinds of freedom instead of one unitary version gives us a broader and truer way of seeing things. In our current world, our new singular view of freedom has begun to cause us problems. That is because we do not fully understand that we are warring against ourselves when we claim sovereign and civic freedoms are harmful.

Although this is the end of this narrative, there is an unending list of new ways to view things in our culture using the new kinds of freedom as contrasted to the simpler concept of constraint removal and applied equality. Those ideas may certainly be the subjects for more books in the future.

Bibliography

Allison, Graham T., *Essence of Decision*. Boston: Little Brown and Company, 1971.

Bloom, Allan, *The Closing of the American Mind*. New York: Simon and Schuster, 1987.

Bloom, Allan, *The Republic of Plato*. New York: Basic Books, 1968.

Boring, Edwin, *A History of Experimental Psychology*. New York: Appleton-Century-Crofts, 1957.

Collins English Dictionary, 2003.

English Dictionary, *WorldReference.com*, 2003.

Fromm, Eric, *Escape From Freedom*. New York: Avon Books, 1941.

Fromm, Eric, *The Sane Society*. New York: Fawcett World Library, 1955.

Fukuyama, Francis, *The Great Disruption*. New York: Simon and Schuster, Inc., 1999.

Fukuyama, Francis, *The End of History and the Last Man*. New York: Simon and Schuster, Inc., 1992.

"Global Survey Reveals Significant Gap in Meeting World's Health Care Needs," *NIMHPress@nih.gov*, November 2008.

Hoffer, Eric, *The True Believer*. New York: Harper and Row, 1951.

Holland, Tom, *Rubicon*. London: Time Warner Book Group UK, 2003.

Howard, Philip K., *The Death of Common Sense*. New York: Random House, 1994.

Kaufman, Walter, *The Portable Nietzsche*. New York: The Viking Press, 1954.

Lowi, Theodore, *The End of Liberalism*. New York: W.W.Norton, 1979.

McKenna, George, *American Politics*. New York: McGraw-Hill, Inc., 1976.

Murphy, Cullen, *Are We Rome?* New York: Houghton Mifflin Company, 2007.

NCES Commissioner, Education Committee, "The State of American Schools," June 2006.

Patterson, Orlando, *Freedom*. New York: HarperCollins Publishers, 1991.

Patterson, Orlando, *Slavery and Social Death*. Cambridge, MA: Harvard University Press, 1982.

Peele, Stanton, *The Diseasing of America*. San Francisco: Jossey-Bass Publishers, 1995.

Reisman, Glazer, Denny, *The Lonely Crowd*. New York: Doubleday Anchor Books, 1953.

Revel, Jean-Francois, *Democracy Against Itself*. New York: The Free Press, 1993.

Rothwax, Harold, *Guilty*. New York: Random House, 1996.

Stanford Encyclopedia of Philosophy (2007 revision).

"Statistical Data, Office of Highway Policy Information, Federal Highway Administration," Highway Statistics 2004.

Szasz, Thomas, S., *The Manufacture of Madness*. New York: Harper and Row, 1970.

The Alliance for Excellent Education, "How does the United States Stack up?" March 2008.

The New Commission of the Skills of the American Work Force, "The Opportunity Equation," June 2009.

Appendix

Sources for Graphs 1, 2, & 3

Japan

Source: Koichi Hamai, senior research officer, First Research Department, Research and Training Institute, Ministry of Justice, Government of Japan translated the data taken from the annual White Paper on Crime. The full citation is: Government of Japan, *Summary of the White Paper on Crime* (Tokyo: Research and Training Institute, Ministry of Justice, annual editions). Japanese Ministry of Health and Welfare, Department of Statistics and Information.

Sweden

Source: Statistics Sweden (Statistika Centralbyran), *Kriminalstatistik* 1994 (Stockholm: Statistics Sweden, 1994). Jean-Paul Sardon, *General Natality* (Paris: National Institute of Demographic Studies, 1994); Fukuyama's personal correspondence, June 11, 1998, Ake Nilsson, Statistics Sweden; *Population Statistics 1996, Part 4, Vital Statistics* (Stockholm: Statistics Sweden, 1997).

United States

Source: Fukuyama's personal correspondence from the Program Support Section, Criminal Justice Information Services Division, Federal Bureau of Investigation, U.S. Department of Justice. Data are obtained on a voluntary

105

106 | Floyd Sours

basis through the Uniform Crime Reporting (UCR) program managed by the FBI. S. J. Ventura, J. A. Martin, T. J. Mathews, and S. C. Clarke, Report of Final Natality Statistics, 1996, Monthly Vital Statistics Report, Vol. 46, #11 supplement (Hyattsville, Md.: National Center for Health Statistics,1998); S. J. Ventura, *Births to Unmarried Mothers: United States, 1980–1992*, National Center for Health Statistics, Vital Health Statistics 21(53) (Hyattsville, Md.: National Center for Health Statistics, 1995; U.S. Department of Health and Human Services, *Vital Statistics of the United States*, Vol. 1: *Natality*, Publication # (PHS) 96-1100 Hyattsville, Md.: National Center for Health Statistics, 1996); S. C. Clarke, *Advance Report of Final Divorce Statistics, 1989 and 1990*, Monthly Vital Statistics Report, Vol. 43, #8 supplement (Hyattsville, Md.: National Center for Health Statistics, 1995); National Center for Health Statistics, *Births, Marriages, Divorces and Deaths for 1996, Monthly Vital Statistics Report,* Vol. 45, #12 (Hyattsville, Md.: National Center for Health Statistics, 1997).

England and Wales

Source: Home Office, *Criminal Statistics: England and Wales* (London: Her Majesty's Stationery Office, various years). United Nations Department for Economic and Social Information and Policy Analysis, *World Population Prospects: The 1996 Revision-Annex 1-Demographic Indicators* (New York: United Nations Publications, 1996); United Nations Department for Economic and Social Information and Policy Analysis, Statistical Division, *Demographic Yearbook,* (New York: United Nations Publications, 1965–1995); Council of Europe, Recent Demographic Developments in Europe (Strasbourg: Council of Europe Publishing, 1997).

INDEX

A

Acorn agency, 60
Adams, John, 46
adversity, 17
alienation, 24, 85
Alliance for Excellent Education, 52
Allison, Graham, 83
  Essence of Decision, 83
America, 38–39, 95
American Political Science Association, 56
American Politics (McKenna), 79
anarchy, 27, 36
antithesis, 94
anxiety, 93
Are We Rome? (Murphy), 58
Athens, ancient, 20
authoritarianism, 19, 24, 28–30, 34–35, 54, 58, 62, 73–74, 79, 94, 96
authority, absolute, 20, 24, 35
autonomousness, 94
awareness, public, 93

B

barbarians, 30
bipartisan, 94
Bloom, Allan, 52, 68
  Closing of the American Mind, The, 52

blurring, 36, 50, 54, 66, 73–74, 83, 90, 94–95
Bosnia, 37
bread and circuses, 23, 59
bull in the china shop metaphor, 70–71, 79

C

Caesar, 43–44
civil rights movement, American, 31
Clinton, Bill, 63
Closing of the American Mind, The (Bloom), 52
coercion, 12, 21, 26, 37, 52, 80, 98
community spirit, 62–63
conflict
  resolution, 63, 82–83
  socialization of, 79
constrain, 33–34
  informal and formal ways to, 34
constraints, 31, 33–34, 36, 47
  civic, 31
  direct, 34
  external, 20, 33, 46, 51, 63
  loosening of, 20, 47, 51, 57, 86
  producing harm, 41
control, 24, 29, 34–36, 41, 61
corruption, 12
  in business, 60
  in government, 60–61

107

in politics, 58
crime rates, 16, 37
Cuban Missile Crisis, 83

D

Death of Common Sense, The
(Howard), 60, 71
decision making, 79
decriminalization, 32, 38, 49–50
democracy, 19, 23–24, 34–36, 45–46,
58, 73–74, 79, 87, 92
discipline, 27, 41, 54, 86
Diseasing of America, The (Peele), 67
disruption, great, 38–40, 49
division of labor, 46
divorce rates. *See* graph, divorce rates
due process, 50

E

education
comparison with other countries,
52–53
traditional, 52–53, 55
educational system, American, 52, 55
elitism, 27, 53
emperor, 23, 45, 59
*End of History and the Last Man,
The* (Fukuyama), 23, 28
End of Liberalism, The (Lowi), 56, 60
enlightenment, 26–27
enterprise, free, 28, 85
equal, 31
equality, 16, 18–19, 23–24, 26–28, 35,
39, 44, 46, 51, 65, 81, 97
legal, 27, 97
Essence of Decision (Allison), 83
ethnic cleansing, 37

F

fair, 31

fear, 52–53
freedom, 16, 18–21, 26–27, 39, 98
definitions of, 13, 19–21
economic, 28
harm of, 28, 89
ideal, 20
individual, 27
kinds of
civic, 19–20, 23, 34, 46, 71
personal, 12, 18–20, 23–24, 27, 33,
35–36, 46, 68, 92, 98
sovereign, 19–21, 23–24, 27, 46, 51
popular, 24, 35
social, 28
yearning of, 30–31
Freedom (Patterson), 20–21
Freedom of speech, 38, 42, 44–45,
80–81, 83
Fukuyama, Francis, 23, 28–30, 38–40,
49, 51
*End of History and the Last Man,
The,* 23, 28
Great Disruption, The, 38, 49

G

glory, 44–45
good and bad, belief in, 16, 51, 69–71,
73–74, 77, 94
governance, 30
authoritarian, 22, 24, 30, 35–36, 80,
92
democratic, 30
totalitarian, 35
government, liberal, 56
graph
divorce rates, 39
theft crime, 38
violent crime, 38
Great Disruption, The (Fukuyama),
38, 49
guilt, 50, 69–71, 73–75, 94

Burnt Offerings | 109

H

harm, 16, 29, 31, 38, 40–41, 45, 47–
    51, 53, 63, 65, 83, 86, 88, 95–96
  cultural, 33, 37, 95
Hegel, Georg Wilhelm Friedrich, 28,
    93–94
Hoffer, Eric, 86
Holland, Tom, 42
  Rubicon, 42, 45
homework, banned, 54
honor, 27–28, 44–45
Howard, Philip, *Death of Common
    Sense, The*, 50–51, 60–61, 68,
    71–73, 78–79
"How Does the United States Stack
    Up?," 52
Hussein, Saddam, 37

I

ideas, free trade in, 80
ideology, 58, 86–88, 90, 93
Ides of March, 44
Imperial Rome, 58–60, 62
incarceration, 50
industrial revolution, 26–27
inequalities, 12, 16, 18, 21, 26–28,
    31–32, 43–44, 46, 50–55, 62–64,
    70–73, 75, 78, 85, 91–92, 95
innocence, 50, 69–71, 73–75, 94
Internet, 16
intimidation, 27, 52–53, 63, 98
Iraq War, 37

J

Japan, 38
journalism, investigative, 77
judgment, bad
  in government, 57, 61, 68, 71, 73
  in politics, 60, 68, 84

K

Kennedy, Robert, 56

L

law, 30, 34–35, 37, 43, 45, 61, 71, 78,
    85, 91
  common, 71, 78
  formal, 51
  statutory, 77–78
liberalism, 56
liberty, 55, 80
lip service, 40
logic, 31
Lonely Crowd, The (Riesman), 94
Lowi, Theodore, 50–51, 56–58, 60–62,
    68, 70–71, 77
  End of Liberalism, The, 56, 60

M

Manufacture of Madness, The
    (Szasz), 64
manumission, 23, 30
master, 21–22, 31, 49, 55, 87, 94. *See
    also* relationship, master-slave
McKenna, George, 79–82
  American Politics, 79
Menendez brothers, 72
mental health, 64, 67–68, 86
  benefits of treatment in, 68
  statistics, 68
murder, 28, 94
Murphy, Cullen, 58–60
  Are We Rome?, 58

N

NCES (National Center for Educational
    Statistics), 52
New Commission of the Skills of the

American Workforce, 52
Nietzsche, Friedrich, 27
Nixon, Richard, 80–81

O

Office of Highway Policy Information, 48
Office of the Federal Register, 79
opinion, public, 19, 55, 62, 80
opposites, dueling, 93

P

patronage, 23, 58–59, 62–63, 78
    American, 58
    government, 60
Patterson, Orlando, 20–23, 30, 54
    Freedom, 20–21
    Slavery and Social Death, 21–22
Peele, Stanton, 67–68
    Diseasing of America, The, 67
Plato (philosopher), 69
Pogo (comic strip character), 76
police force, 43
politics, small groups in, 79
power
    absolute, 23–24
    as a thing that corrupts, 96
prejudice, racial, 74
prestige, 28, 53
privatization, 60
problem resolution, 71, 93–95
progress, 19, 26, 31, 56, 88, 90, 95
prosperity, 19, 28, 58, 85
Protestant revolution, 26
punishment, 17, 33, 37, 43, 50, 53, 75, 98

R

racism, 74–75
Reagan, Ronald, 63

reasoning, modern and traditional, 32
reciprocity, 62–63, 78
recognition, 28, 37, 53, 78, 81, 93
regression, belated, 36
relationship
    between freedom of speech and
        decision making, 79
    doctor-patient, 64
    master-slave, 21–23, 28–30, 35, 44, 54
    predator-victim, 28–29, 36
    teacher-student, 52, 54
    therapist-counselor, 64
resentment, 31
restrain, 33–34
restraints, 33
Riesman, David, 94
    Lonely Crowd, The, 94
rigidity, 36, 73–74, 93–94
Roman Republic, ancient, 42, 96
Rubicon (Holland), 42, 45

S

science, 27, 31–32, 35
    modern, 19, 26
Second Republic of the United States, 56
self-esteem, 28, 55–56, 86
Simpson, O. J., 74–75
"Six Blind Men and an Elephant," 7
slavery, 19–21, 23, 28
Slavery and Social Death (Patterson), 21–22
slaves, 19, 21–22, 33, 35, 49, 93–94. *See also* relationship, master-slave
social engineering, 37
sovereign, rigid, 36
specialization, 43, 46
speech, freedom of, 79–81, 83
status, 27, 37, 53, 81
strength, 43–44
structure, 22, 33–34, 47, 62, 85, 93

suffragium, 58
synthesis, 94
Szasz, Thomas, 64, 66
  Manufacture of Madness, The, 64

T

technological innovation, 26–27, 31,
    40, 46, 56
thesis, 94
totalitarianism, 30

V

vertical hierarchies, 30–31, 44, 51–53,
    60, 63

W

war, 28–29, 36, 90, 94
Watergate affair, 79–80, 82–83

Z

Zeitgeist, 16, 27

Edwards Brothers,Inc!
Thorofare, NJ 08086
01 July, 2010
BA2010182